Lernkrimi Englisch

Death Comes Knocking

Oliver Astley
Barry Hamilton

Compact Verlag

Inhalt

Redaktion: Helga Aichele
Fachredaktion: Nathalie Russell
Produktion: Wolfram Friedrich
Titelillustration: Karl Knospe
Typographischer Entwurf: EKH Werbeagentur GbR
Umschlaggestaltung: Carsten Abelbeck

ISBN 978-3-8174-7945-0
7279451

Besuchen Sie uns im Internet: www.compactverlag.de, www.lernkrimi.de

Vorwort

„Die Compact Lernkrimis mit ihrer Kombination aus Lektüre und didaktischem Übungsanteil eignen sich hervorragend, um breite Sprachkompetenzen in der Fremdsprache zu erwerben. Der Selbstlerner wird dabei durch die spannende Handlung, das angemessene Sprachniveau und den stetig ansteigenden Schwierigkeitsgrad der Übungen gefördert und motiviert."

Prof. Dr. Christiane Neveling, Didaktik der romanischen Sprachen, Universität Leipzig

Liebe Leserin, lieber Leser,

Sie möchten Ihr Englisch verbessern? Congratulations! Mit diesem Lernkrimi werden Sie Ihre Englischkenntnisse quasi mühelos erweitern und Ihre Sprachkompetenz motiviert trainieren. Denn das Compact Lernkrimi-Konzept, entwickelt nach neuesten Erkenntnissen der Fremdsprachendidaktik und evaluiert durch Prof. Dr. Christiane Neveling (Universität Leipzig), bringt Sie sicher zum Lernerfolg – mit Spaß und Spannung! Durch die Kombination aus didaktisierter Lektüre und ausgewählten Übungen knüpfen Sie an Ihr individuelles Sprachniveau an und setzen eigene Schwerpunkte für Ihre persönlichen Lernziele. In variationsreichen Übungen mit engem Textbezug machen Sie sich Ihre Lernprozesse bewusst und erweitern Ihre Wortschatz- und Grammatikkenntnisse nach und nach in Modulen. Am Ende des Buches können Sie Ihr Wissen in einem Abschlusstest selbst überprüfen. Ein Glossar mit zentralen Wörtern, die im Text hervorgehoben sind, hilft Ihnen bei der eigenständigen Lektüre.

Bauen Sie Ihr Wissen aus: Das modulare System der Reihe Compact Lernkrimi ermöglicht es Ihnen, Ihr Lernprogramm abwechslungsreich und effektiv zu ge-

stalten. Eine Übersicht aller Lernkrimis finden Sie auf den letzten Seiten dieses Buches. Die in den Krimis angebotenen Lernbereiche Grundwortschatz, Aufbauwortschatz, Grammatik und Konversation sowie die Einteilung nach den Niveaustufen des Europäischen Referenzrahmens helfen Ihnen bei der Auswahl des passenden Buchs. Neben den Lektüretiteln bieten Ihnen die Lernkrimi-Reihen mit CD (Hörbuch, Sprachkurs, Audio-Learning) zusätzliches Training Ihres Hörverstehens und Ihrer Sprechfertigkeit.
Compact Lernkrimis sind somit das ideale Medium für einen Lernerfolg im Selbststudium. Durch die kleinen Texteinheiten und den hohen Übungsanteil sind sie aber auch als Unterrichtslektüre bestens geeignet.

So lernen Sie mit Compact Lernkrimis:

- **Unabhängig sein:** Pensum und Geschwindigkeit beim Sprachenlernen individuell wählen – unabhängig von Kursinhalten oder wöchentlichen Terminen.
- **Mit Begeisterung lernen:** Sprach- und Landeskenntnisse kontextualisiert festigen, angeregt durch einen spannenden Text, der in die Kultur des Zielsprachenlandes eingebettet ist.
- **Wissen intensivieren und erweitern:** In über 60 Übungsaufgaben mit ansteigendem Schwierigkeitsgrad lexikalische und grammatikalische Kenntnisse trainieren und erweitern.
- **Systematisch lernen:** Mit dem modularen System individuelle Lernziele setzen – linear im Schwierigkeitsgrad ansteigend oder mit punktuellen Schwerpunkten – und den persönlichen Lernweg verfolgen.
- **Wissen evaluieren:** Das eigene Wissen selbstständig im Abschlusstest überprüfen – und sich anhand der Analyse neue Ziele stecken und künftige Trainingsschwerpunkte formulieren.

Tauchen Sie ein in eine spannende Krimistory und trainieren Sie Ihr Englisch auf unterhaltsame Art und Weise. Lernkrimis des Compact Verlags führen Sie step by step zum Lese- und Lernerfolg!

Viel Spaß beim
spannend Englisch lernen
wünschen Ihnen

Prof. Dr. Christiane Neveling
und die Compact Lernkrimi-Redaktion

Death Comes Knocking

Oliver Astley

1 A Fright in the Night

Everyone knew everything about everyone in Llanprid, a charming old village in the middle of Wales. Many of the residents were related, most were friendly towards each other, and those who were neither friends nor relatives loved gossiping about each other.
The same families had lived in the same houses for at least three generations, and young lovers often strengthened the close-knit community by getting married. Few people decided to move away forever. Those who did were usually the black sheep of the family.
One example was Peter Wallis, the adopted son of Catherine Wallis. Everyone knew he was not really a Wallis, but nobody knew his real surname. Even the other children in Llanprid had not accepted the strange, tall boy who had arrived in their village when he was nine years old. He had always been an outsider, and he was happy to leave the place almost ten years later when he began studying law at university. Since then, he had never looked back.
Peter did not stay in close contact with anyone in the village apart from Catherine. After all, she was the nearest thing he had to family. And Catherine, who was very proud of her son, never tired of telling her neighbours about his achievements. This made it difficult for the other residents of Llanprid to forget about Peter Wallis, that

residents	Einwohner
to gossip	tratschen
close-knit community	enge Gemeinschaft
to tire of doing sth.	müde werden, etw. zu tun
achievements	Leistungen

unusually quiet person who always dressed in black.

Now in his mid-thirties, Peter was a successful lawyer in Cardiff. Although he did not have the time to visit Catherine very often, he **kept in touch** on the telephone, and he sent a postcard whenever he went on holiday.

to keep in touch	in Verbindung bleiben
shaky	zittrig
to get hold of sb.	jmd. erreichen
to put the kettle on	Wasser aufsetzen
only child	Einzelkind

At the start of their conversation one early Sunday evening, Peter noticed that his mother sounded very upset.

"Oh, Peter!" she began, "I'm so glad I could reach you."

Catherine did not usually call on Sundays because that was the day Peter rang her; his mother's turn was on Wednesdays. They always spoke after her favourite television programme ended at 9 p.m. This was something that had simply become a tradition.

"You know I always have my mobile with me," he answered. "I was going to call you later. Is everything all right, Mum?"

"No, not really," she replied in a **shaky** voice. "It's not all right at all. There were some horrible noises coming from upstairs earlier, and they started again a few moments ago… I can't **get hold of** any of the neighbours. I don't know what to do!"

"Try to relax, Mum," said Peter calmly. "**Put the kettle on** and tell me what you mean."

Peter could remember growing up in that old cottage. He had been an **only child**, but there had been lots of spiders and mice to play with. Some of the neighbours' cats often came round as well, either to eat the food he put out in the back garden for them or to hunt fresh mice for themselves. It meant that there were always funny noises coming from somewhere. But his mother was certain that she could hear a human voice this time, and that someone was laughing and calling her name.

"It sounded like Cyril!" she told him.

"I'm sure there's nobody else in the house," he replied. "How could there be? You always lock the doors, don't you?"

Catherine agreed, and before the kettle had even started whistling she was beginning to sound a little more relaxed. Talking to Peter helped her to **think straight**, and he was right about one thing: living alone since the **divorce** had made her very nervous.

"I only have to hear the doorbell ring and I almost **jump out of my skin**," she joked. "My poor heart will be the death of me."

A long time ago, the Wallises had been one of the largest families in Llanprid. Nature was not on their side, though: many of Catherine's relatives had died of **heart failure** before they reached the age of forty.

"That's how I lost both my mother and your uncle," she remembered aloud and **sighed**.

Übung 1: Fill in the blanks. Lesen Sie weiter und ergänzen Sie den Text mit dem passenden Wort!

front | doorbell | neighbours | surprise

Suddenly the 1. ____________ rang and Catherine jumped up in 2. ____________ .

"Oh! Just a minute, dear," she said. "There's someone at the 3. ____________ door."

"Do you really think you should answer it?" asked Peter.

"Yes, it'll be one of the 4. ____________ . I left a message with Mary asking her to come round. I'll call you later."

Peter paused again and finally agreed, "Okay, Mum."
"Goodbye, dear!" she said and hung up.
Catherine picked up her **cane** and began walking towards the front door. On her way, she was **startled** by a loud knocking from the other side of the house. It sounded as if there was somebody at the back door. Was it possible? She'd just been sitting there in the kitchen.
"Who's there?" she called.
There was no answer from either side of the house, but again a knocking came from the back door. Three loud bangs filled the small cottage. The knocking was so strong that Catherine could hear the **china** plates next to the sink dancing from side to side. Her heart began to race.

to think straight	klar denken
divorce	Scheidung
ϟ to jump out of one's skin	erschreckt hochfahren
heart failure	Herzversagen
to sigh	seufzen
cane	Spazierstock
to startle sb.	jmd. erschrecken
china	Porzellan
to shuffle	schlurfen
shape	Gestalt, Form

Maybe Peter was right, she thought. She shouldn't open the door to anyone, just in case.
"Who is it?" she shouted again nervously.
"Hello, Cathy! Is everything all right?" asked a familiar voice from the other side of the back door.
Finally! There was only one person who called her "Cathy". She turned around and **shuffled** along the corridor and back into the kitchen. A **shape** moved behind the glass. Catherine felt much safer knowing that someone had come to keep her company.
The kettle was whistling loudly now; she would make them both a nice cup of tea.
After turning the key in the lock with a shaky hand, she opened the door.

Übung 2: Translation. Übersetzen Sie die Wendungen aus dem Text!

1. Ist alles in Ordnung? ______________________
2. nur für alle Fälle ______________________
3. ein bekannte Stimme ______________________
4. die Porzellanteller ______________________

"Thank heavens you're here," she began. "It's been such a..."
She fell silent when she saw the face looking back at her. It was not the familiar[i] face she was expecting, but a white, **expressionless** mask. Her eyes opened wide and her heart began to beat even faster. The voice that came from inside was as dark and frightening as the empty, black eyes staring straight at her.

False Friends

familiar ≠ familiär
familiar = bekannt, vertraut
personal, informal = familiär

"Such a scary evening?" it **mocked**.

expression-less	ausdruckslos
to mock	spotten
chest	Brust
sweat	Schweiß
pointless	zwecklos
to witness	miterleben, Zeuge sein von
entire	ganz, gesamt

Catherine dropped her cane and put both hands over her mouth. Her heart seemed to stop beating in her **chest**. Her skin was suddenly covered in a cold **sweat**. She tried to step back into the kitchen, but the dark figure moved too quickly.
All the old woman could do was panic and look around helplessly for someone to save her. She tried to scream, but it was **pointless**; she had no breath to scream.

Moments later, Catherine Wallis' lifeless body was lying on the cold kitchen floor. Her dead eyes stared at the ceiling in horror. On top of the cooker, the steaming kettle was jumping and screaming as if it had **witnessed** the **entire** scene.

Übung 3: Multiple choice. Welcher Satz ist korrekt? Kreuzen Sie an!

1. a) ❒ Peter's Catherines adopted son.
   b) ❒ Peter's Catherine's adopted son.

2. a) ❒ He helped her thinking straight.
   b) ❒ He helped her to think straight.

3. a) ❒ There was a loud knocking at the door.
   b) ❒ It knocked loudly at the door.

4. a) ❒ Catherine was death on the floor.
   b) ❒ Catherine was dead on the floor.

2 The Man in Black

Raven Close was a typical road for an old village. It ran along the edge of John Bidderscum's farm, so one side was **lined with** trees and a very thick **hedge**. On the other side there was a row of houses, each of which had a small front garden. In the summer these gardens were full of colourful plants and flowers, but now, by late October, the ground was covered with brown leaves.

lined with	gesäumt von
hedge	Hecke
ϟ battle-axe	Dragoner, (alter) Drachen
to distract	ablenken

Catherine Wallis lived next door to a woman whose back garden looked like a jungle. Her name was Mary Giles, and – as she always used to tell the young postman – she could not look after the house because of her bad leg.

The postman was one of the few people who regularly spoke to Miss Giles. She was a lonely pensioner who had argued with every family on Raven Close over the years. The only real friends she had left were her cats – and Catherine, who liked the old woman's strong personality and lovingly called her "the old **battle-axe**".

When Miss Giles stepped outside to call in Theodor, one of her cats, the whistling coming from her neighbour's house made her stop and listen. Seconds later, her attention was suddenly **distracted** by something moving in the long grass in her garden. She thought it was her missing cat.

"Theodor? The-o-dor! Dinner!" she shouted.

A dark figure that was at least twenty times larger than Theodor stood up on two legs, ran up the garden and disappeared through a hole in Miss Giles' fence. She **gasped** and hurried back into her house, forgetting all about the whistling.

to gasp	keuchen, nach Luft schnappen
to wonder	sich fragen
to hobble	hinken
to give out	*hier*: von sich geben
flashing	blinkend, aufleuchtend
paramedic	Rettungssanitäter

When ten minutes later Theodor had still not scratched at the door to be let in, the old woman opened her door to call him again. Immediately she heard the whistling noise again and **wondered** what it could be.
Miss Giles **hobbled** across to the hedge that separated her garden from Catherine's and noticed that her neighbour's back door was wide open. That was strange, she thought. Suddenly she saw a hand lying in the doorway and **gave out** a horrified scream.

Übung 4: Opposites. Lesen Sie weiter und unterstreichen Sie die Gegenteile der angegebenen Wörter!

departed | in the middle | bored | before | behind | nodding

The ambulance arrived first on Raven Close and parked on the side of the road. The **flashing** blue lights brought several interested faces to windows and doors. The neighbours wanted to see what was going on at the Wallis cottage.
Shortly afterwards, a police car parked in front of the same house and two officers in uniform stepped out of the vehicle. One of the **paramedics** walked up to them, shaking his head, and invited them both inside.

Within ten minutes the front door opened again, and the two officers left the cottage. They put on their hats and made their way next door to the woman who had called the ambulance.

Some of the villagers recognized Inspector Davies, the tall, thin man with grey hair who knocked on Miss Giles' door. Nobody knew the **plump** officer who was with him, though.

"I knew something bad was going to happen to that poor woman," Miss Giles said mysteriously as soon as she opened the door. "I can see these things."

Inspector Davies **blinked** at the woman, who paused to look at him over her thick, black glasses before she continued.

plump	pummelig
to blink	blinzeln
superior	Vorgesetzter
to wipe	abwischen
tartly	bissig, mit scharfer Zunge
to knit	stricken

"I can," she said knowingly. "I read Catherine's tea leaves only last week. There was a clear picture of a cross at the bottom of the cup, as well as a fork, a heart and the letter J."

"What does that mean?" the young officer asked her politely.

"It means nothing at all," her **superior** answered brusquely. "Can Sergeant Jones and I come inside to talk to you, Miss Giles?"

"You can come in," she answered, "but **wipe** your shoes first."

It was almost 9 p.m. when the police began interviewing Miss Giles, and they were still listening to her long stories over half an hour later.

"Please let's concentrate on the facts," said Inspector Davies in a tired voice. "Can you describe the person you saw in your garden just before you called the ambulance?"

"It was a big man, that's all I can tell you for certain," she replied. "Oh, and he was wearing black. That much was clear when he got up and ran away. My outside light was on."

"Are you sure it was a man, Miss Giles?" asked Sergeant Jones.
"Absolutely. He was at least six feet tall, and there are no women around here like that," she said a little **tartly**.
Inspector Davies smiled slightly and asked his next question: "Can you think of anyone who may have wanted to hurt Mrs Wallis?"
The old woman gave a sharp laugh.
"Let me tell you one thing, Inspector," she answered. "Catherine Wallis was a sweet, kind lady. She was harmless, and everyone loved her – apart from that Cyril, of course."
The inspector looked at the woman, expecting further details, but she picked up some wool and began to **knit**.

Übung 5: Reading comprehension. Beantworten Sie die Fragen zum Text!

1. Who called the ambulance?

___

2. How is the person in the garden described?

___

3. Which of the two police officers is thinner?

___

4. What did Miss Giles do to see Catherine's future?

___

"Miss Giles," Inspector Davies said calmly, "we need to know everything you know about **the deceased** that could be important. We cannot be certain yet what, or who, caused her death."

"Then you should go and speak to Cyril Rogers yourself," she **muttered**. "The less I talk about that man the better." (i)

> **the ... the ...**
> Vergleichssätze nach dem Muster **je ... desto ...** werden im Englischen mit **the** + Komparativ **the** + Komparativ wiedergegeben, z. B.: **the bigger the better.** Es wird also die erste Steigerungsform des Adjektives verwendet. Die Wortstellung ist dabei die des normalen Aussagesatzes.

Sergeant Jones looked at her notes. Miss Giles had already told them a few basic details about Catherine Wallis, including her family history. She had mentioned Cyril Rogers' name a couple of times before: he was Mrs Wallis' ex-husband.

A couple of hours later that same evening, the police finally found somebody in at Cyril's house, but they were not given a warm welcome.

the deceased	der/die Verstorbene
to mutter	murmeln, nuscheln
to grumble	murren, brummen
unshaven	unrasiert
flatly	ausdruckslos
to be lost for words	sprachlos sein

"What time do you call this?" **grumbled** a very tall, **unshaven** man.

He obviously had not noticed the uniform of the young woman standing in front of him. His cheeks and nose were bright red, and his breath smelled strongly of beer.

"Mr Rogers? I'm sorry to disturb you," said Sergeant Jones politely, "but I'm afraid we have some bad news about your ex-wife."

"Cathy? I know she's dead," he replied **flatly**. "Everybody was talking about it at the pub tonight. Is that all you wanted to tell me?"

Inspector Davies and Sergeant Jones **were lost for words**. Cyril Rogers did not appear to be at all upset about Catherine's death.

"It's very tragic, of course… so sudden," he added when he saw that the two were studying his face very closely.
"We're still trying to find out exactly what happened," explained the inspector. "Is it okay if we ask you a few questions?"
Cyril suddenly looked a little worried. He **swallowed** nervously and asked the question that was on his mind: "You don't think someone killed her, do you?"
"It's too soon to say whether the death is **suspicious** or not. However, a witness saw someone dressed in black near Mrs Wallis' house earlier this evening, and we would like to find out who that was," Inspector Davies explained.

to swallow	schlucken
suspicious	verdächtig
to divorce	sich scheiden lassen

Cyril did not respond. His eyes were like glass.
"Were you at the pub all evening, Mr Rogers?"
"Of course! I stayed there after the rugby with all the boys."
Cyril Rogers was not an athletic man, and at the age of fifty-six he was not a boy either. But the Welsh rugby team had played against Ireland in the afternoon, and most of the sports fans in Llanprid went to watch such matches on the large television screen at The Red Dragon.
"You should speak to the Stevens family if you haven't done that yet," he said before Inspector Davies could ask his next question. "Their young boy James is nothing but trouble."
Sergeant Jones made a note of the Stevens' address and told Cyril that they would definitely visit every family in the area.
"Is it right that you **divorced** Mrs Wallis only a month ago, Mr Rogers?" Inspector Davies asked.
Cyril moved his eyes from the sergeant's notebook to the inspector and gave him an angry look.
"It became official in September, yes," he replied shortly. "But we've been separated for over two years."

"And you left her for another woman, if I understand correctly," the inspector continued.

"Look, if you want to **accuse me of** something, just say it!" Cyril **snapped**.

"Nobody is accusing anyone of anything, Mr Rogers," Inspector Davies replied in a calm voice. "We're just finding out everything we can about your ex-wife."

Sergeant Jones watched the two men exchange looks. They were staring at each other as if they were trying to **read each other's minds** during a game of **chess**.

"I left her for another woman, but the two of us are not together any more. Catherine was quite ill," said Cyril slowly. "I'm very sorry that she's dead, but it's not a big surprise."

He repeated what Inspector Davies had already learnt about Mrs Wallis: she had needed a **pacemaker** and had taken tablets because of a weak heart.

to accuse sb. of sth.	jmd. etwas vorwerfen
to snap	*hier*: blaffen
to read sb.'s mind	jds. Gedanken lesen
chess	Schach
pacemaker	Herzschrittmacher
to slam	zuschlagen

"Did you see each other very often?" the inspector continued.

"Yes, sure," Cyril said, nodding. "You can't hide from anyone in a village this small, but we had nothing to say to each other most of the time."

A woman's voice from upstairs called Cyril's name.

"Look, can we talk about this tomorrow?" he asked. "Thanks for coming round, but I don't think I can help you."

Sergeant Jones was about to say something when Inspector Davies put his hand on her arm.

"That's fine, Mr Rogers," he said pleasantly. "You have a good night and we'll continue our questions here or at the station tomorrow.

Here's my card. Just give me a call if there's anything you want to tell me in the morning."
Cyril **slammed** the door shut without even saying goodnight and hurried upstairs to the voice that was still calling him.

Übung 6: Phrasal verbs. Ordnen Sie den Wörtern die passende Definition zu!

1. ☐ hang up	**a)** find boring
2. ☐ tire of	**b)** visit
3. ☐ come round	**c)** contact
4. ☐ get hold of	**d)** end a telephone call

3 The Grim Reaper

On the following morning, a large crowd of people had gathered again outside the Wallis cottage. Sergeant Jones arrived and looked at the house. The front wall was a strange pink colour, which she had not noticed the night before. It seemed as if half the residents of Llanprid were there, although all they could see was a lot of parked cars and some tape around the house. The forensics team was busy at work inside.

It was the most exciting thing that had happened in the village since John Bidderscum, the man who owned the farm across the road, accidentally drove his tractor into Catherine Wallis' front garden. Everybody was gossiping about the night before and Cyril Rogers' many reasons for wanting to get rid of his ex-wife.

Sergeant Jones was among the crowd. She had tried to find people in their houses, but most of them were either at work or standing at the end of Raven Close. There was a lot of information to collect, so she was hectically taking notes as the villagers competed with each other to speak.

"Cyril hated Catherine," said one voice, "and they were always arguing with each other."

"That's right," another person agreed. "I remember a fight they had only last month. Very nasty, it

the Grim Reaper	der Sensenmann
forensics	Spurensicherung
accidentally	versehentlich, unbeabsichtigt
to compete	wetteifern
disapproving	missbilligend

was. I'm sure Cyril said he would kill Catherine if she came anywhere near his house again..."

Suddenly everyone stopped talking and turned their heads towards Cyril Rogers' house down the road. The front door opened and a very tall woman stepped outside. She closed the door, looked at the crowd, paused for a moment, then crossed the road in the opposite direction.

"That's Vivienne Gray," whispered one of the old ladies. "She must be Cyril's new partner. She's half his age!"

"Isn't she with Bidderscum's youngest, the postman?"

"Just look at her!" said another woman in a disapproving voice. "That woman's all legs and no heart. How can anyone wear such a tiny skirt on a cold and windy day, I ask you?"

Sergeant Jones saw Vivienne Gray look back over her shoulder at the group of people. This was someone she definitely wanted to talk to, she thought.

"I'll be back in a few minutes, ladies," she said and ran after the woman.

Übung 7: Odd one out. Welches Wort ist das „schwarze Schaf"? Unterstreichen Sie das nicht in die Reihe passende Wort!

1. planned intentionally accidentally knowingly
2. heart lungs brain skeleton
3. unlock close slam shut
4. flat expressionless unemotional excited

Meanwhile, Inspector Davies was organizing the **investigation** at the police station in the nearby town of Welshpool. Catherine Wallis' body was at the **mortuary**. Peter Wallis, the **next of kin**, was coming to Llanprid; the police in Cardiff had contacted him on Sunday night.

investigation	Ermittlung, Untersuchung
mortuary	Leichenhalle
next of kin	nächster Angehöriger
pointy	spitz
injury	Verletzung
forced entry	gewaltsames Eindringen
to frown	die Stirn runzeln
weeds	Unkraut

In over twenty years with the police, the inspector had not worked on many murder cases. Such serious crimes were not common in the countryside, but things did not look good on Raven Close.

Inspector Davies was sitting at his desk eating an egg sandwich when the forensics expert entered his office. She was a very serious woman with short, black hair and a **pointy** nose. Her face always reminded the inspector of a crow.

"Ah, hello Jenny," he said. "Have you brought me some news about Catherine Wallis?"

"There's very little to tell you, Stewart," she answered. "There's no sign of **injury** on the body and there was definitely no **forced entry** into the house. The kitchen's clean; it looks like nobody had been in there apart from the deceased."

Inspector Davies took another bite from his sandwich.

"What about the person Miss Giles saw in her garden?" he asked with a full mouth.

Jenny **frowned** and pulled out some photographs from a brown envelope.

"There's nothing obvious yet," she said. "But you've seen what the team has to look at, haven't you? There are dead leaves everywhere, and the **weeds** in the neighbour's garden have grown almost as tall as a man. It will be some time before they finish collecting **evidence**."

evidence	Beweis
suspect	Verdächtiger
apparently	angeblich, anscheinend
trace	Spur

The inspector sighed and asked when the autopsy was going to take place. It was impossible to investigate a death without knowing for sure whether murder was involved. And at this point he had no weapon, no motive, and no real **suspect**.

At that moment the telephone rang. It was Sergeant Jones; she had finished interviewing the residents of Raven Close. Jenny pointed at her watch to say that she was busy.

"Tomorrow," she whispered and walked away.

He nodded and listened to what Sergeant Jones had to report: most of the families had been at home or at The Red Dragon on Sunday evening, she explained, and nobody apart from Miss Giles had seen a suspicious person dressed in black. Mr and Mrs Stevens were **apparently** on holiday, and there was no **trace** of their son James.

Übung 8: Tenses. Setzen Sie die Verben in der korrekten Zeitform ein!

read   investigate   search   work

1. Right now they __________ the garden for evidence.
2. She will be tired if she __________ all night.
3. The sergeant __________ many murders before.
4. I __________ this book for over two weeks now.

"There is one thing, though, sir," Sergeant Jones said after the inspector sighed again.
"Oh? What's that, then?" he asked, suddenly interested.
"Well, it's about Cyril Rogers. He told us last night that he had spent the entire evening at the pub with his friends, but that wasn't true."
"Not true, you say?" the inspector repeated.
"No, sir. Well, he was there all right, but he left for around an hour between 7:30 and 8:30. And that's not all..."
"Go on, Jones," Inspector Davies said after swallowing the last mouthful of his egg sandwich. "I'm listening."

incident	Vorfall, Ereignis
to offend sb.	jmd. beleidigen
hanging basket	Blumenampel
a blazing row	ein furchtbarer Streit
pansy	Stiefmütterchen

"People have seen him and Mrs Wallis arguing recently. They didn't speak for a while because their lawyers were writing a lot of letters, but there have been a couple of **incidents** since the divorce."
"What do you mean by 'incidents'?"
"Well, it's a bit childish, really. Mr Rogers' new girlfriend **offended** Mrs Wallis in the post office last month, and so she cut off all the [i] heads of the flowers in his **hanging baskets** later that day. There was **a blazing row** when he caught her."
"I see," said the inspector flatly but with a smile on his face. "And do you think that someone's life is worth a few **pansies**?"
"Of course not, sir," she replied. "But Cyril's words were very clear. He said, 'I'll kill you if you come anywhere near my house again.'"
"Well, he does seem to be an aggressive man," he agreed.
Inspector Davies was about to ask Sergeant Jones to bring Cyril

> **All the ...** bezeichnet eine eingeschränkte, bestimmte Menge, **all** ohne Artikel wird dagegen in allgemeinen Aussagen verwendet,
> z. B. All women like flowers.

Rogers to the station for questioning when the receptionist came around the corner with that very person beside him.
"Oh, speak of the devil! I'll call you back later, Jones," he said and raised his eyebrows at the two men who had just entered the room.
"Gentlemen?"
"A Mr Rogers from Llanprid to see you, Inspector," announced the receptionist. "He said he urgently needs to speak to the person **in charge of** the Catherine Wallis case."
Cyril Rogers walked up to Inspector Davies' desk and dropped a plastic bag on the table. It contained what looked like a large playing card.
"What do you make of that, then?" he asked without saying hello.

in charge of	zuständig für
threat	Drohung, Bedrohung
scythe	Sense
solemn	düster

The inspector slowly looked at both sides of the card.
"Where did you find this?" he asked.
"Someone put it through my letterbox this morning," Cyril answered. "It's clearly a **threat**!"
The card showed a skeleton dressed in a black robe and holding a long **scythe**; at the top was a number in Roman numerals.
"Oh dear," Inspector Davies said, his eyes fixed on Cyril's, "number thirteen. That's unlucky for some, isn't it?"
It had been a long time since the inspector had seen a tarot card. This one was the most famous one, though. And almost everyone knows the **solemn** picture of Death – or the Grim Reaper, as he is also known.
"Did you receive a note or anything else with this, Mr Rogers?" the inspector continued.
"No, nothing at all. Why?"
"Well, obviously it would help us identify where the card came from. Do you have any idea who might have a reason to threaten you?"

Cyril looked alarmed. "No! Anyone could have delivered it," he snapped.
"I see. Well, never mind. We'll have the card examined and see what we can find."
"Is that all you have to say?" Cyril demanded in a loud voice. "Isn't it obvious that somebody wants me dead?"
Inspector Davies scratched the back of his head and told the man that he was welcome to stay at the station for a few hours if he felt that his life was in danger. In any case, they would have something important to discuss as soon as Sergeant Jones returned from the village.

Later that day, an expensive car turned into Raven Close and parked opposite the Wallis cottage. Nosy faces watched the driver getting out of the vehicle from their living room windows. It was a tall man in a smart, black suit. Most people recognized him immediately when he stood up and turned around. They had not seen him for several years, but there was no question about it: it was Peter Wallis.

Übung 9: Unscramble. Lesen Sie weiter und bilden Sie sinnvolle Wörter aus dem Buchstabenchaos!

Peter looked at the faces in the windows from the other side of the road. A few heads were **1.** dingond ______________ at him in sympathy.

"Come here, you poor thing!" a **2.** eicov ______________ suddenly said behind him.

As Peter turned, Miss Giles put her thin arms around him.

She had just left her house and was still **3.** ginrycar ______________ her knitting. The long needles **poked** him in the back.

The **4.** scorefins ______________ team was still busy examining his mother's cottage and the two gardens, so Peter went next door to speak with his old **5.** roughbien ______________.

"Make yourself comfortable, dear," Miss Giles said as they passed the kitchen door. "I'll put the kettle on and we can have a good chat."

The **peculiar** smell of Miss Giles' house made Peter feel like he was a child again. He saw that the sofas were covered in cat hair and decided to sit down at the living room table. Whenever he looked out of the window, he saw four people walking around in white suits.

nosy	neugierig
smart	*hier*: schick
sympathy	Mitgefühl
to poke	stechen
peculiar	seltsam
windowsill	Fensterbank
wrinkly	runzlig

Theodor, one of the oldest cats, was sitting between two black and white photographs on the **windowsill** and staring at a spider.

"You still have a lovely house, Miss Giles," he lied as she carried a tray of tea into the living room.

The old woman was not interested in talking about herself. Instead, she kept saying how shocked she was about Catherine's death and told Peter all about the questions that the police had asked.

"You have a difficult road ahead," she said and pressed her cold, **wrinkly** hand against his.

Before he realized what she was doing, Miss Giles had put on her thick glasses and was **reading his palm**.

to read sb.'s palm	jmd. aus der Hand lesen
bad luck	Pech
deck	*hier*: Kartenspiel

"But I see a happy future for you, eventually," she explained. "You will have a long and successful life and many children to share it with."

Peter smiled politely. He had heard the same story several years ago when Miss Giles had last tried to tell his fortune.

"You're not going to get out your tarot cards, too, are you?" he joked.

Miss Giles took off her glasses and put them down on the table.

"Of course not, dear," she smiled. "There's a card missing, and it's **bad luck** to use an incomplete **deck**."

Übung 10: Translation quiz. Übersetzen Sie und enträtseln Sie das Lösungswort!

1. Stiefmütterchen □ _ _ _ _
2. Menschenmenge _ _ □ _ _
3. Fensterbrett _ _ _ _ _ _ _ _ □ _
4. Verletzung □ _ _ _ _ _
5. vorwerfen _ _ □ _ _ _
6. beleidigen _ _ _ □ _ _

Lösung: □ □ □ □ □ □

4 Ghosts

Cyril Rogers left the police station with a red face. He had changed his alibi for Sunday evening to include the hour or so he had spent with Vivienne Gray. He could not remember the exact times. Inspector Davies remained sceptical.

"The two of them could be working together," he suggested to Sergeant Jones, who was adding the report from the forensics department to the **case file**.

"They both fit Miss Giles' description," she added. "After all, all she saw was a tall person dressed in black. We have no idea if it was really a man or a woman."

The inspector muttered something about the bad eyesight of old people and that she had probably imagined the whole thing.

"What about their motive, though?" he continued.

case file	Fallakte
will	Testament

"I'm not sure, sir, but I've been thinking about that. Mrs Wallis had no children with Mr Rogers, and she changed her name two years ago, a long time before the divorce was final. She probably left everything to her adopted son."

"I see," said the inspector. "I'll see what I can find out about her **will**."

"What about the death threat that Mr Rogers received?" Sergeant Jones asked. "Do you think someone could have a reason to kill both him and Mrs Wallis?"

"I wouldn't be surprised if he was inventing the whole thing to make himself appear innocent," the inspector said. "He didn't tell us about his arguments with Mrs Wallis, and he was very quick to accuse James Stevens. We should definitely **observe** that man very closely. In that way, we'll either be **protecting** him, or we might catch him."

Back in Llanprid, Peter Wallis was searching for an excuse to **turn down** a third cup of tea when somebody knocked loudly at the front door.
"I'll get it," he said to Miss Giles.
Peter walked along the hallway, taking care not to step on the cats as he went.

Übung 11: Unscramble the text. Lesen Sie weiter und bringen Sie die folgenden Sätze in die richtige Reihenfolge!

a) "Terribly sorry to hear about your poor mum," he said. "Very sad news, it was. Everyone in the village is thinking of you."

b) "Hello there," said the man in a cheerful voice. "**Long time, no see!**"

c) "Who's there?" Miss Giles called from the other side of the house. She sounded like an old **witch** when she shouted so loudly.

d) He opened the door and did not recognize the man on the other side.

1	2	3	4

"It's John!" the man shouted back and smiled nervously at Peter, who obviously had no idea who John was.
"You've really grown up, Peter! You're almost as tall as me now."
Peter couldn't think of anything to say but showed the visitor into the living room, where he offered him some tea from the pot.
"I thought you were that Cyril Rogers," said Miss Giles. "You sound just like him, you know."
"Oh yes, people often tell us both that."
It became clear through the conversation of the two villagers that the man was John Bidderscum, the farmer who owned the field on the other side of Raven Close.
"Anyway, Mary, you're probably wondering why I came over," John announced, suddenly changing the subject.
Peter saw the farmer look out of the window for the third time. He seemed distracted by the forensics team.

to observe	beobachten
to protect	(be)schützen
to turn sth. down	etw. ablehnen
ϟ Long time, no see!	Lange nicht gesehen!
witch	Hexe
to sort out	*hier*: in Ordnung bringen
to bother sb.	*hier*: jmd. beschäftigen

"I've been telling you for a long time that I would come and **sort out** your garden, so I thought I would do it today before the weather turns bad. It will be winter soon."
Miss Giles was very happy to hear this, but there was an obvious problem that Peter was quick to mention: the police were still at work in her back garden.
"I can see that!" replied John. "I can start around the front, though, and you can let me know when the police have finished whatever it is they need to do. I've brought everything I need."
John Bidderscum went back outside and began unloading his van. Moments later, Peter asked the old woman a question that had been **bothering him**.

"Why's he being so friendly? Everyone here hates the Bidderscums, don't they?"
"No, dear!" she **exclaimed**. "What makes you think that? They're a very nice family, especially John and his wife."
"I don't know… something my mum told me once, I **suppose**."
"Oh, well – yes. Your poor mother didn't like him very much, but the Wallises and the Bidderscums have always fought like cat and dog. John was here yesterday as well, you know. He promised he would repair the television **aerial** on my roof. He looked a bit tired, but he said he didn't mind. I'm always telling his son how difficult it is for me to look after the place. Do you remember Gareth, their youngest? He's the village postman now."
Peter had stopped listening to Miss Giles. He remembered that the police in Cardiff had told him to call an Inspector Davies when he arrived in Llanprid: he had to arrange a time to look around his mother's cottage and see whether anything had been stolen.

Übung 12: Translation. Übersetzen Sie folgende Sätze!

1. Wir lassen den Brief morgen untersuchen.

____

2. Gestern Abend wollte er ihr Gesellschaft leisten.

____

3. Soll ich jetzt das Wasser aufsetzen?

____

4. Leider sieht die alte Dame sehr schlecht.

____

It was the last day of October, and heavy rain in the late afternoon made John stop working in the front garden just as the sky began to grow dark. That was very atmospheric for Hallowe'en, he thought. He put his **tools** into his van and told Miss Giles that he was going to buy some food in town and asked if she needed anything.

Further down the road, James Stevens was preparing the biggest party of his life. His parents were still on holiday in Egypt, and he **intended** to **make the most of** their large house. Everyone at the local high school knew that he was throwing a Hallowe'en party. Those with an invitation had planned their costumes weeks ago.

to exclaim	ausrufen
to suppose	annehmen, vermuten
aerial	Antenne
tool	Werkzeug
to intend	beabsichtigen
to make the most of sth.	das Beste machen aus
valuable	wertvoll
haunted castle	Spukschloss
cobweb	Spinnennetz
to put the final touches to sth.	etw. den letzten Schliff geben
to snigger	(hämisch) kichern

James had had a very busy day. First he had locked away anything **valuable** that his friends could break or steal, then he and his two best friends had spent hours making the house look like a **haunted castle**. Candles were already burning on the windowsills, and all of the rooms contained spooky decorations and **cobwebs**. There was also a skeleton that the boys had stolen from the biology room at school.

Once the work was done, they began **putting the final touches to** their costumes before the first guests arrived.

"Have you invited the neighbours?" asked Count Dracula.

James smiled innocently. "Of course I have! Something tells me they won't come, though."

"That's a shame!" laughed Frankenstein's monster. "This party's going to be wild! All those pensioners would be a good catch."

James **sniggered** and picked up his plastic scythe.

"Yeah, they would," he agreed. "But even Death needs to have a night off and relax sometimes!"
He placed a white mask over his face and pulled his black **hood** over the top of his head.

Later that evening, Sergeant Jones and one of her junior colleagues were observing Cyril Rogers. They were sitting in an **unmarked car** outside The Red Dragon. It was raining heavily.
The suspect and his girlfriend had entered the pub arm in arm less than an hour ago. The whole village knew by now that he and Vivienne Gray were together, so they were being much less discreet about their relationship.

hood	Kapuze
unmarked car	Zivilfahrzeug (der Polizei)
to sob	schluchzen
unmistakable	unverwechselbar
screeching brakes	quietschende Bremsen

Suddenly, the door opened and Cyril ran around the side of the building. He sat down on a step and began to **sob**, his face buried in his arms.
Seconds later, Sergeant Jones' attention moved from Cyril Rogers to her colleague's camera, which was pointed at a tall figure leaving the pub. The long legs were **unmistakable**: Vivienne Gray was marching away in the opposite direction.
"Oh dear, Tom!" the sergeant said, somewhat[i] amused. "It looks like there's trouble in paradise. I wonder if their alibi will last as long as their relationship?"
At that moment the sound of **screeching brakes** filled the air. A car had come to an abrupt stop just outside The Red Dragon where Vivienne had been crossing the road.

> Das zusammengesetzte Adverb **somewhat** (etwas, ein wenig) wird analog zu **somehow** oder **sometimes** verwendet, um einen unbestimmten Grad zu bezeichnen.

Übung 13: Word forms. Ergänzen Sie das jeweilige Adverb und Substantiv!

1. heavy ____________ ____________
2. suspicious ____________ ____________
3. helpless ____________ ____________
4. innocent ____________ ____________

"You crazy idiot!" shouted an angry woman. "You could have killed me!"

Cyril recognized Vivienne's voice and got up to see what was going on. Sergeant Jones sent Tom after him to investigate. Tom **pretended** to be an ordinary **passer-by**.

"What happened here?" he asked. "Is everyone all right?"

"No!" shouted Vivienne in a shaky voice. "He tried to hit me!"

"What a load of nonsense," replied the driver shortly.

to pretend	so tun, als ob; vorgeben
passer-by	Passant
to run sb. over	jmd. überfahren

The driver was the man whom Tom had seen working in Miss Giles' garden that afternoon. He listened to the two arguing while Cyril silently watched on with an open mouth. Vivienne had been going out with one of the man's sons, Gareth, and she was accusing him of trying to **run her over** like a dog.

5 Revenge

The first morning of November was the start of a busy day for Inspector Davies. The autopsy results for Catherine Wallis arrived before noon, and it was confirmed that she had died of natural causes.

"Heart failure," he told Sergeant Jones without expression.

"But we know there's more to it than that, sir!" she objected.

"Yes, and our young lawyer from Cardiff knows that, too," he replied. "Let's try to stick to the facts here."

The inspector scratched his head and began to summarize his conversation with the son.

"Peter is the executor of his mother's will. Both he and Cyril knew that Catherine had left everything to Peter, even though Cyril had to give a lot to Catherine after the divorce. Are you with me so far?"

"Yes, I see," the sergeant said. "What else did he have to tell you?"

"Now then, on Sunday evening he stopped talking to his mother when somebody visited her. She told him that a neighbour was at the door and hung up."

"A neighbour?" Sergeant Jones asked in surprise.

"Yes. According to Peter, Catherine had left a message on Miss Giles' answering machine; she had also spoken to a woman at Mr Rogers' house."

"Vivienne? But Catherine couldn't stand her or Cyril!"

"I know," the inspector replied. "She sounded very frightened on the phone. She said she'd heard Cyril upstairs at around 6 p.m."

"But he was at the pub. That makes no sense!" Sergeant Jones said.

"Well, those are the facts. It's our job to make sense of them."

The inspector showed her the case file.

"The forensics team found some black **fibres** in Miss Giles' garden where our mystery person climbed over the hedge," he said.

"I don't know if that will help us unless we find someone wearing torn clothes," she smiled.

to die of natural causes	eines natürlichen Todes sterben
to object	einwenden
executor	Testamentsvollstrecker, Nachlassverwalter
fibre	Faser
to recreate	nachbilden
to rummage around	herumwühlen
muddy puddle	Schlammpfütze
encouragingly	ermutigend

"Well, quite. They also discovered a number of footprints. The rain has destroyed most of the evidence, but they're working to **recreate** an entire footprint."

"What kind of footprint are we looking at?"

Inspector Davies **rummaged around** on his desk and pulled out a brown envelope from a pile of papers. Inside there were three photographs showing what appeared to be **muddy puddles** and a length of measuring tape.

"Apparently our man wears size twelve or thirteen shoes. That's all we know."

"Pretty big! We know we're looking for a man, then," said Sergeant Jones **encouragingly**. "That's something, at least."

Their first visit that afternoon was to Cyril Rogers' house. He was as polite as ever when he opened the door.

"What the hell do you want this time?" he snapped.

Cyril found it amusing that the police wanted to look at his shoes, and he did not understand why they were disappointed when he showed them that he wore a size eight.

"Never mind his shoes, Inspector," said a tart voice. "What are you going to do about that madman up the road who tried to kill me?"
It was Vivienne Gray, dressed in a black bathrobe. Apparently she and Cyril had **settled** their **differences**, thought Sergeant Jones.
"Ah, Miss Gray," the inspector replied, "I believe you forgot to tell my colleague that you'd spoken to Mrs Wallis shortly before her death."
"That's right, I forgot!" she said. "Well, it was a very short call."
Inspector Davies frowned but asked her to describe yesterday's incident with John Bidderscum outside the pub. Sergeant Jones had not yet mentioned it because of all the other developments at the station that morning. He listened politely at first, but he soon tired of the village politics. After all, nobody had been injured.

Übung 14: Choose the correct alternative. Lesen Sie weiter und unterstreichen Sie die richtige Variante!

The pair next stopped at a house that had **severed** heads **1.** in / on the windowsills. Cyril had **2.** said / told the police that James Stevens was definitely back in the village: only a **deaf** person **3.** would have / could have ignored the party those kids were having last night, he **4.** said / had said angrily.

The teenager who opened the door smiled **sheepishly** at the police.
While Sergeant Jones was speaking, the inspector looked him over from head to toe. The boy was a giant and his feet were huge.

"Can you tell us where you were between 7 p.m. and 9 p.m. on Sunday evening?" she asked.

"Erm...," James Stevens said after a pause, "oh yeah, I was bowling in Welshpool."

The sergeant noted down some details and said they would be in touch.

to settle differences	Differenzen beilegen
severed	abgetrennt
deaf	taub
sheepishly	einfältig
to flick through	durchblättern
neatly	ordentlich, sauber
laundry basket	Wäschekorb
to approach	sich nähern

"We'll have to check the boy's alibi before we question him," Inspector Davies said as they walked up the road to Miss Giles' house. "But I'm more interested in John Bidderscum now. Have you already spoken to him? He sounds as loud and aggressive as Cyril Rogers!"

Sergeant Jones **flicked through** her black book, stopped at a page with a lot of **neatly** written notes and smiled.

"Oh yes, he was very pleasant, actually. He gave me a lot of details, but none of them seemed very important. Let's see... on Sunday he returned from a fishing trip in the evening and went straight to bed."

At the top of the hill, they could see Miss Giles' front garden. It was very tidy, although someone had apparently emptied their **laundry basket** onto the grass. As they **approached**, the inspector saw that the colourful pile was in fact a number of cats lying on the lawn.

The old lady watched the police arrive from her living room window and invited them in. She seemed to be rather nervous.

"Let me come to the point, Miss Giles," said the inspector the minute she began with her usual small talk. "Mrs Wallis told her son that she left you a message on Sunday. Do you remember that?"

"A message? No, I've not received one for days, and it's impossible to ignore the flashing red light. I'm not blind, you know!"

At that moment her television crackled and the picture disappeared. "Oh, no!" the old woman cried. "How am I going to watch my soaps now? It was only two days ago that John fixed the aerial."

> Mit der typisch britischen Wendung **ever so** wird in der Umgangssprache eine Aussage verstärkt. Z. B.: ever so many - sehr viele, ever so slightly - ein ganz klein wenig

Inspector Davies frowned and asked how often the man visited. "Oh, he's been an angel ever since that accident with the tractor," she said. "Do you know he ruined Catherine's lovely garden and destroyed my rockery? He was ever so (i) upset about it all."

The inspector was trying to make sense of the weekend's events. "Did you leave Mr Bidderscum alone in your house on Sunday?"

"No," she said, thinking. "Well, only when I was looking for Theodor."

There was a short pause in which both police officers exchanged a meaningful look. It was long enough to miss a phone call.

"Do you mind if I have a look upstairs, Miss Giles?" the inspector suddenly asked. "Sergeant Jones will keep you company here."

Übung 15: Fill in the blanks. Lesen Sie weiter und setzen Sie die fehlenden Wörter ein!

The **1.** s________ smiled reassuringly when **2.** h________ superior disappeared up the **3.** s________. She asked Miss Giles whether Mr Bidderscum also used to visit Mrs Wallis from time to **4.** t________. The old lady laughed.

"Now there's a story!" she said happily. "The Bidderscums and the Wallises don't get along very well at all. It must be in the blood. There was a **family feud** for generations when there were more of them. They were always fighting or competing to **outdo** each other, and dear old Catherine was very proud of her family's history."
Miss Giles made some tea and began talking about the Wallis family, many of whom had died at a young age. Inspector Davies then returned and whispered something into his colleague's ear.
"Think very carefully," began Sergeant Jones. "Did Mrs Wallis do anything recently that might have upset John Bidderscum?"
There was a short pause.
"Well," began Miss Giles, "there was that whole business with the cottage, I suppose. Catherine had the front of her house painted last week. You must have noticed that it's a funny **shade** of pink."

to crackle	knacken, knistern
rockery	Steingarten
reassuringly	beruhigend
family feud	Familienfehde
to outdo sb.	jmd. übertreffen
shade	*hier*: Farbton, Schattierung
to change hands	den Besitzer wechseln

"Why would that have upset Mr Bidderscum?" the inspector asked impatiently.
"That's obvious," she said in her tart voice. "The Wallises have lived in that house for only two or three generations. The Bidderscums used to live there before that, you see – some of them, anyway. It was Robert Bidderscum who built the cottage back in the 1870s..."
Miss Giles picked up a photograph from the windowsill.
"That's him there with my grandfather," she explained.
"So the cottage **changed hands** at some point?" asked the sergeant.
Miss Giles nodded and told them that Catherine's mother had moved into the house with a Bidderscum after he married for a second time. It was a long and complicated story.

"In short, some of the older Bidderscums might feel that the house is still **rightfully** theirs, if I understand it correctly," the inspector said.
"Just imagine seeing 'your' house painted a strange pink colour one day," added Sergeant Jones **ominously**.
Miss Giles' face **lit up**.
"Oh, he was **furious**! Now you mention it, I remember him making quite a few comments. I won't repeat words like that, though."
Inspector Davies smiled innocently and thanked the old woman.
"You've been very helpful," he said, "but we must **be off** now."
Miss Giles watched the police leave, then she shuffled across the living room to the table. She picked up her incomplete deck of tarot cards and threw them into the **bin**.
"I thought I was in trouble then, Theodor!" she said to the cat. "At least I gave that Cyril Rogers a little fright!"

Übung 16: Questions. Ergänzen Sie das richtige Frage-wort!

1. __________ about your promise to help me?

2. __________ about telling me everything from the start?

3. __________ does he come to visit you?

4. __________ do you like your tea, Inspector?

John Bidderscum was singing when the police found him feeding the pigs on his farm. He was standing up to his ankles in mud.
"Please don't talk to me about Vivienne Gray," he sighed when the

inspector asked him to explain what had happened on the previous night. "I'm quite busy, and I've got no time for that **slut**."
Inspector Davies was surprised by the man's language.
"Sorry," the farmer continued, "but she broke my young **lad's** heart."
"Maybe we could talk about your visits to Mary Giles, then," the inspector said.
John smiled and explained that he tried to be a good neighbour.
"And you wanted to keep an eye on what the police were doing."
The man turned and looked at the inspector, who had picked up one of the large, dirty **trainers** that were on the wall next to the **pigsty**.

rightfully	rechtmäßig
ominously	unheilvoll
to light up	*hier*: aufleuchten, strahlen
furious	sehr wütend
to be off	*hier*: weggehen
bin	Mülleimer
⚡ slut	Schlampe
⚡ lad	Bursche, Junge
trainers	*hier*: Turnschuhe
pigsty	Schweinestall
to freeze	*hier*: erstarren
loft	Dachboden

"Miss Giles has already destroyed your alibi for Sunday," Inspector Davies said. "I wonder if this shoe matches the footprints we found."
John **froze** for a moment and replied, "I don't know what you mean."
The inspector continued to explain that he knew that Mr Bidderscum had fixed Miss Giles' aerial on Sunday, and that it was possible to enter Mrs Wallis' **loft** from her neighbour's house.
"Peter Wallis told us that his mother heard a voice up there. She didn't know who it was, but I think we might have the answer.
The farmer looked very serious and walked out of the pigsty.
"I didn't mean to kill her!" he objected. "Sure, I wanted to frighten her a little, but I'd forgotten that the old girl had such a weak heart."

"We'll see about that," said Inspector Davies ominously. "I think we should go to the station now and talk this over in detail, don't you?"

A few days later, Miss Giles was reading the local newspaper when she saw the headline about Catherine Wallis and dropped her spoon.

It read: "Llanprid Pensioner Scared to Death."

"It all makes sense to me, Theodor," she told her cat. "The heart, the farmer's fork, the letter J for John… I saw it all in her tea leaves."

The Secret of Crowroad Castle

Barry Hamilton

1 A Happy Family

James Tate and his **newly-wed** wife, Joanne Tate, were driving in a brand new, shiny Jaguar along a road in the Scottish Highlands. It wasn't exactly what one would call a golden autumn day. To their left a **loch** lay under a grey sky. Raindrops were falling, breaking up the loch's **smooth**, dark-black surface.

"They all hate me!" **exclaimed** Joanne Tate in an American accent.

"Now, now dear – I think you're **exaggerating**," said her husband.

"What's wrong with being 31 years younger than your husband?" said Joanne Tate aggressively.

"I imagine they think you're after my money, darling," he replied.

Joanne Tate **sighed**. "They're always so **prejudiced**, these upper-class British families!"

"But you do like my money, don't you darling?" grinned James Tate.

"Of course! However, as you know, I have enough of my own," she smiled.

newly-wed	frisch verheiratet
loch	See (Schottland)
smooth	glatt
to exclaim	ausrufen
to exaggerate	übertreiben
to sigh	seufzen
prejudiced	voreingenommen
cattle	Rinder, Vieh
drawing room	Salon, Wohnzimmer
blurred	*hier*: beschlagen
to approach	sich nähern
⚡ to screw up one's nose	die Nase rümpfen

The newly-wed couple were on their way to Crowroad Castle in the Scottish Highlands. It was about an hour's drive from Glasgow. The castle had belonged to the Tates – a very powerful and rich

British family – for many generations now. Once a year the whole family met in the castle to talk about the family business. The castle was the home of Grace Tate, who was the head of the family. Grace Tate and many other members of the family had not been happy when they heard of the marriage. They thought it was a scandal that James Tate had married such a young blonde American from Texas. They already called her "the cowgirl" behind her back because her father owned several **cattle** farms.
"Here we are!" said James Tate as he drove the car through a large black gate.
In the distance one could see Crowroad Castle.
"That castle looks like one out of a horror movie," Joanne Tate said.
Her husband laughed. "Well, this time you're not too far from the truth!"

Übung 1: Fill in the blanks. Lesen Sie den Text weiter und setzen Sie die angegebenen Begriffe richtig ein!

moment | castle | understatement | stepmother | window

Lara Tate, a very attractive young woman, was looking out of the castle's **drawing room** 1. ______, which was **blurred** with rain. She watched her father's Jaguar **approach** the 2. ______ and stop in front of the house. The 3. ______ she saw Joanne Tate step out of the car, Lara **screwed up her nose**. She was only one year younger than her 4. ______ and to say she did not like her father's new wife would be an 5. ______.

Lara Tate had no real reason for disliking her. Maybe she just felt the "cowgirl" was an **insult** to her **late** mother's memory.
Joanne Tate's shoes were so high she could hardly walk on the **gravel drive**. Lara Tate smiled when she saw her stepmother nearly fall. Just at that moment, her grandmother, Grace Tate, appeared beside her granddaughter.
"She looks **awfully** out of place, don't you think, my dear?" Grace Tate said in her typical cold, upper-class English accent.
Although over eighty, Grace Tate seemed to have the strength and health of a 50-year-old. She was a strict and **ruthless** woman, who also enjoyed sticking her nose into other people's business.

James Tate entered the drawing room with Joanne just behind him and greeted his mother with a kiss on either cheek. Then he saw Lara standing by the window.
"Lara, my darling, how lovely to see you!" James Tate called across the drawing room in a loud, friendly voice.
He walked **swiftly** towards his daughter and greeted her warmly. Grace Tate greeted Joanne kindly, but also a little arrogantly. Lara looked over to Joanne and smiled unkindly.
"What a surprise! I thought you had some cows to look after?" she asked sarcastically.
"No, funnily enough they know how to behave. Which is more than I can say about some people I know," Joanne Tate replied.
"Now, now girls!" a nice voice said from the door.
The voice belonged to Georgina Tate, the daughter of Grace Tate and James' sister. She was carrying a tray with champagne glasses.
"I think it's time for a drink," she added.

insult	Beleidigung
late	*hier*: (kürzlich) verstorben
gravel drive	Kiesauffahrt
awfully	furchtbar
ruthless	umbarmherzig
swiftly	rasch, schnell

James Tate, who never knew how to handle the constant fighting between his wife and his daughter, rubbed his hands cheerfully. "What a **jolly good** idea, Georgina!"
Georgina Tate gave out the glasses. She and her mother were the only ones who actually lived in the castle all year round. Georgina was a **spinster** and worked as a personal secretary for her mother. This seemed to be her only **purpose in life**. Some people said she was a **slave** to her mother.
"Cheers!" said James Tate **jovially**. Everybody lifted their glasses. "Cheers!"
"To another successful year of excellent family business," said Grace Tate.

ϟ jolly good	prima, hervorragend
ϟ spinster	unverheiratete Frau, alte Jungfer
purpose in life	Lebensziel
slave	Sklave/Sklavin
jovially	fröhlich, herzlich
sip	Schlückchen
to deserve	verdienen

Joanne Tate drank her champagne quickly while Georgina Tate just took a little **sip** of hers.
"Where is Aunt Valeria?" asked Lara Tate.
"Heaven knows!" her grandmother sighed. "She's probably waiting for her husband to finish spending all her money on horse racing."
"But he's jolly good at it, grandmother," said Lara. "He gave me a tip once and I won quite a bit of money."
"Well, that's probably all he's jolly good at," said Grace Tate quietly.
Valeria McPherson was Grace Tate's youngest daughter and was married to Daniel McPherson. Until he had married into the Tate family, he had been a simple car mechanic. Grace Tate did not like that at all – her daughter **deserved** much better.
Suddenly the doorbell rang.
"Oh, that will be them!" Georgina exclaimed.
"Yes, talk of the devil…," said Grace.

She nodded at her daughter, and Georgina immediately walked towards the door.

Übung 2: Opposites. Finden Sie das passende Gegenteil und setzen Sie die richtige Ziffer ein!

1.	☐ cheerful	a) clear
2.	☐ ruthless	b) unhappy
3.	☐ blurred	c) low
4.	☐ high	d) kind

"She's well trained," Joanna Tate whispered in her husband's ear. "Yes," he replied quietly. "Better than a dog!"

Soon a man in his early thirties entered the drawing room. Daniel McPherson was wearing an expensive jacket, a white shirt, jeans and **trainers**. He was a very friendly and charming man. Nevertheless, he was more tolerated than liked by most of the Tates. Only Lara Tate seemed to like him. And obviously his wife Valeria loved him.

trainers	*hier*: Turnschuhe
ϟ folks	Leute
collar	*hier*: Halsband

"Good afternoon, **folks**!" Daniel McPherson said in a strong Scottish accent.

He was followed by his wife, who was wearing a pink designer suit. In one hand she held a gold handbag and in the other a dog lead, which was connected to the silver **collar** of a small black poodle. The dog did not really want to enter the room and was pulling at the lead.

"It's okay, Babushka, no one will hurt you. They are all nice people in here."
"That damn thing bit my finger last time!" whispered James Tate to his wife. "I nearly **drowned** it in the loch!"

Later on at dinner, the Tates discussed family business. They had just finished their starter and were waiting for the main course to be served. James Tate **dabbed** his lips with his **napkin**.
"But we really could do with the money," he said. "My factory needs to invest in new machines."
"As I pointed out before, James, I don't have any to give," his mother replied.
"But if you don't, we might go bankrupt!" he said **agitatedly**.
"Well, you should have run the business more **economically**!" she answered coldly.

to drown sb.	jmd. ertränken
to dab	abtupfen
napkin	Stoffserviette
agitatedly	aufgeregt, aufgewühlt
economically	wirtschaftlich, sparsam

Übung 3: Verb forms. Ergänzen Sie Simple Past und Past Participle der folgenden Verben!

1. dab ____________ ____________
2. get ____________ ____________
3. go ____________ ____________
4. see ____________ ____________
5. wear ____________ ____________

James Tate got up suddenly from his chair and angrily threw his napkin on the table.

"I must say, you certainly run our family business like a dictator! I don't know how long I'll **put up with** this!" he exclaimed and left the dining room.

For a moment it was silent. Then Grace Tate smiled dryly.

"Well, I think it's time for the second course," [i] she said. "Georgina, would you mind?"

Georgina hesitated.

"Are you all right, my dear?" her mother asked.

"Yes, it was just… I was **wondering**…," said Georgina Tate nervously.

"Yes?" asked Grace Tate a little impatiently.

"Did you think about my holidays? I told you I wanted to go to Spain… I've never really been on holiday and I thought…"

"Now why would you need to go on holiday, my dear? We have everything here that you need to relax: A beautiful loch, lovely hills and superb landscapes."

"But…," her daughter **insisted**.

"Georgina, we would really like to have our main course. Could you please make sure we get it?" Grace Tate said **sternly**. "One could die of hunger with the time you're taking!"

Without another word, Georgina Tate left the dining room. There was another **uneasy** silence. After this unsuccessful dinner, nobody was really in the mood for sherry and cognac afterwards, so most of the Tate family went to bed early.

> Im Zusammenhang mit einer Mahlzeit bezeichnet **course** einen Gang in der Menüfolge. Der **second course** ist also der zweite Gang, **main course** der Hauptgang.

to put up with sth.	etw. tolerieren
to wonder	sich fragen
to insist	beharren, bestehen auf
sternly	streng
uneasy	unangenehm, ungut

2 Murder at Breakfast Time

The next morning the whole castle was in an uproar. Grace Tate had disappeared. The whole family had searched for her everywhere, but in vain. After several hours of searching, Lara was nervously walking up and down the drawing room. James was staring into the large fireplace.

"It's not like grandmother to just go away without saying anything," said Lara.

"No, it certainly isn't," agreed her father.

Suddenly there was a loud scream outside. James and his daughter ran out of the castle. They quickly found the place where the scream had come from. Georgina Tate stood trembling by the loch. She pointed to the water and there everyone saw a horrible sight: Grace Tate's lifeless body floating in the loch.

in an uproar	in Aufruhr
in vain	vergeblich
trembling	zitternd
horrible sight	schrecklicher Anblick
to float	treiben, schwimmen
moustache	Schnurrbart
crime scene	Tatort

It did not take long for Inspector MacAlister and his assistant, Sergeant O'Neil from the Strathclyde Police, to arrive. The inspector was a tall, slim man with a black moustache. His sergeant was slightly smaller and had a fiery red beard. They stood by Grace Tate's body while the forensic team was busy securing the crime scene. The old woman looked very

small and frail. It was difficult to imagine that she had been the head of a large family enterprise.
"What a horrible way to die," the sergeant said.
"I've seen worse," his superior replied with a sigh.
The inspector turned his attention towards the coroner.
"So what do you think, Miles?" he asked.
The coroner bent down and pointed at Grace Tate's head.
"She received a blow to the head, right here."
"Did it kill her?" the inspector wanted to know.
"Probably, it looks pretty deadly to me."
"So she was killed and then thrown into the water?"
"Yes, or she fell. Depending on where she was standing at the time of the blow."
"What was she hit by?" asked the sergeant.
The coroner looked at the wound on the head again. There were small traces of wood.

Übung 4: Synonyms. Ordnen Sie die Begriffe mit gleichen Bedeutungen einander zu!

1.	☐ horrible	**a)** tremble
2.	☐ shiver	**b)** get
3.	☐ corpse	**c)** awful
4.	☐ receive	**d)** body

"It looks as if the murderer probably used quite a heavy branch."
"So the murder weapon might be quite difficult to find?" the inspector wanted to know.

"Yes, it probably is."

The coroner pointed at the many branches which were lying around.

"It could be that branch or that one or even that one," he said.

"Well, I'm sure you'll try your best to find the right one."

"'Best is not good enough' is what I like to say," the coroner answered with a smile.

"One last thing," said the inspector. "When did she die?"

"She can't have been dead all that long. I would say she probably died some time in the early morning hours."

frail	gebrechlich
superior	Vorgesetzter
coroner	Gerichts-mediziner
blow	Schlag
trace	Spur
Keep me posted!	Halte mich auf dem Laufenden!
to interrogate	befragen, verhören
to nudge	anstubsen
to clear one's throat	sich räuspern

"Well, thanks for now. **Keep me posted**," said Inspector MacAlister.

He looked back at the sergeant.

"Ready for the castle? I think it's time to **interrogate** the Tates."

Shortly afterwards, the two policemen walked into the large drawing room. The men greeted the Tate family, who all looked shocked and sad. Sergeant O'Neil had never been in a castle before in which people actually really lived, so he could not help looking around curiously. Inspector MacAlister **nudged** his sergeant gently with his elbow. This woke Sergeant O'Neil up out of his trance and he took out his pencil and notebook. Although he did not show it, the truth was that Inspector MacAlister was just as impressed as the sergeant. He had grown up in a very poor part of Glasgow, living in a flat not even half the size of the Tate's drawing room. And this with his five sisters! He **cleared his throat.**

"I know this is not easy, but I have to ask some important questions… First of all, I would like to know who saw Mrs Tate last?" the inspector asked.

You can say that again!	Das kannst du laut sagen!
to mutter	nuscheln, murmeln
gulp	(großer) Schluck
How dare you!	Wie können Sie es wagen!
procedure	Vorgehensweise

"I did," replied Georgina Tate. "I took her to bed at around 11 p.m."
"Did you notice anything unusual or strange about her?"
"No, she was her usual self."
"**You can say that again!**" **muttered** James Tate.
"What was that?" asked Inspector MacAlister.
"What my husband meant was that his mother was no different to how she usually was," Joanne Tate said, coming to his rescue.
"When did you notice Mrs Tate was missing?" Inspector MacAlister asked.
Georgina Tate answered: "I brought Mother her breakfast this morning at 7:30, as I do every day. But she wasn't in her room. I went looking for her and asked the others if anybody had seen her. But nobody had and we couldn't find her anywhere… And then…"
Georgina Tate was trying hard to hold back her tears. The inspector paused for a moment. Daniel McPherson took a large **gulp** of his whisky. He appeared to be a little nervous, the inspector noticed.
"So where was everybody during the night of Mrs Tate's murder?" continued Inspector MacAlister.
"What are you trying to say here? That one of us killed her? **How dare you!**" exclaimed Valeria McPherson.
She started to cry.
"It's just standard police **procedure**," said Sergeant O'Neil.
"So now back to my question. Miss Tate, you said you brought your mother her breakfast this morning at 7:30?"
Georgina Tate nodded.

Übung 5: **Choose the correct word. Lesen Sie weiter und unterstreichen Sie die richtige Variante!**

"Okay, so where was **1.** everybody / anybody between 11:00 last night and 7:30 this morning? And did anybody notice anything strange during the night?"

"I saw Lara cross the grounds in the early **2.** hours / times this morning," Joanne Tate suddenly said.

"That is a lie, you **bitch**!" Lara shouted across the room at her stepmother.

"It's strange you should say that...," Valeria McPherson interrupted, looking **3.** street / straight over to Joanne Tate. "I saw you leaving your room in the middle of the night."

"That's not true!" Joanne said, **4.** defending / offending herself. "Was Daniel with you all night?"

Daniel McPherson quickly **poured** himself another whisky.
"Of course he was! But I saw you, Joanne!"
"And what were you doing walking about in the middle of the night?" James asked his sister.
"I was going to the loo, if you must know!" Valeria replied angrily.
"Well, so was I!" said Joanne.
Inspector MacAlister **stroked** his moustache.
"Happy families," he quietly said to Sergeant O'Neil.

⚡ bitch	Schlampe
to pour sb. sth.	jmd. etw. einschenken
to stroke	streichen über, streicheln

The sergeant nodded in agreement while he was trying to write down everything that was being said.
"I don't think this is going to get us anywhere, Sergeant," he said.
"I totally agree, sir! My fingers are starting to hurt."

cardigan	Strickjacke
landing stage	Bootssteg
bank	*hier*: Ufer
judging by ...	nach ... zu urteilen
to gasp	nach Luft schnappen, keuchen
apparently	anscheinend, angeblich

"Could you please get some discipline in here?" asked the inspector.
"Of course, sir."
Then he suddenly shouted: "Silence!"
Everybody went silent. Valeria McPherson's poodle hid under the table. It was so quiet you could have heard a pin drop.
"Well, thank you, Sergeant," said Inspector MacAlister, who was slightly surprised by his assistant's drastic intervention.
Suddenly the coroner entered the drawing room and signalled for the inspector to come over to him. Inspector MacAlister excused himself and walked over.
"I have just found this in one of Grace Tate's cardigan pockets," said Miles.
He gave the inspector a wet, but still readable, hand-written note. It read: "Meet me by the landing stage at 7:00 a.m."
"I also went to the landing stage to see if I could find anything helpful...," the coroner informed the inspector.
"And?"
"Well, I found Grace Tate's footprints on the bank just beside the landing stage. It looks as though that was the place where she was hit on the head. Judging by the footprints and the wound, she must have been facing the murderer when he or she hit her. After the blow, she must have fallen into the water. It gets deep

very fast, so that could explain why her body was found somewhere else."

"Or she was pushed out so that her body would not be found straight away."

"That is also a possibility," agreed Miles.

"Well, thank you!" Inspector MacAlister said and walked back into the drawing room.

"Tell me, who was closest to Mrs Tate?" the inspector said to everybody in the room.

"That would be me," [i] answered Georgina Tate. "I am... I mean... I was her personal assistant and also lived here in the castle with her."

"I see," Inspector MacAlister said thoughtfully.

He gave her the note.

"Is this her handwriting?"

"No, but I certainly recognize the handwriting," she **gasped** in surprise.

> That would be me. – Das bin wohl ich.
> Durch die Verwendung eines modalen Hilfsverbs wie **would/might** etc. wird die Gültigkeit einer Aussage eingeschränkt. Der Sprecher vermittelt die Aussage als persönliche Ansicht.
> Die gleiche Funktion erfüllen Satzeinleitungen wie **I guess** oder Adverbien wie **probably.**

"You do?" asked Inspector MacAlister.

"Yes, I actually know the handwriting very well. It belongs to our former butler, Mortimer Grey."

"You said he was your former butler?"

"Yes, Mother fired him a couple of months ago because **apparently** he had sold inside information about the family to a big newspaper."

"I see," said the inspector. "Do you know where I can find him?"

"No, but if he killed my mother, hopefully in hell!" Georgina replied and broke into tears.

Inspector MacAlister excused himself and took his sergeant aside. They walked out of the drawing room.

Übung 6: Questions and answers. Setzen Sie die richtigen Fragepronomen ein und beantworten Sie die Fragen auf Englisch!

Whose | Where | Who | What

1. ______ was closest to the murder victim?

______

2. ______ did they interrogate the Tates?

______

3. ______ happened to the butler?

______

4. ______ handwriting is on the note?

______

So what do you think about all of this, Sergeant?" the inspector asked quietly once they had left the room.

"Well, the information we are getting out of them right now is certainly rather confusing. Everybody is blaming everybody else for something."

"Yes, I think we'll need to question them one by one – up at the police station if necessary," stated the inspector. "But first of all, Sergeant, I suggest we try to find out where this butler lives and pay him a visit."

The sergeant nodded and the inspector walked back into the drawing room.
"Well, I know it's been a very hard day for you all, so we would like to finish our questioning for now. However, I would like to point out that nobody can leave the area until we say so."
Nobody protested. The Tate family accepted quietly what the inspector had just said.

Just as the policemen were walking out of the castle door, Sergeant O'Neil noticed a digital camera hanging over the arm of a **suit of armour.**
"Look at this, sir," he said to the inspector.

to blame sb.	jmd. beschuldigen
to state	feststellen
suit of armour	Ritterrüstung
clue	Spur, Hinweis

"We've got no time for taking photographs," said the inspector.
The sergeant took it off the armour and switched it on.
"There might be some **clues** on it."
"What, you mean the murderer took a picture of himself while he was killing Grace Tate?" the inspector joked.
Sergeant O'Neil went through the pictures. Inspector MacAlister looked at the pictures, too. There were a lot of pictures from the evening before, but nothing really of interest.
"That's an expensive top!" said Sergeant O'Neil looking at a picture of Joanne Tate in a silver and gold top. "My daughter would kill for something like that!"
Suddenly they heard footsteps approaching. Sergeant O'Neil hurried to put the camera back. Then the policemen walked swiftly towards the exit. Inspector MacAlister turned around just in time to see Lara Tate taking her camera off the armour.

3 Did the Butler Do It?

Two hours later, Inspector MacAlister and Sergeant O'Neil were standing in front of a dirty-grey coloured, run-down council house. It had not been difficult to find Mortimer Grey.

"Must have been quite a shock for the butler, moving from a castle into this hole," the sergeant commented on the shabby house in front of them.

"Yes, because he was fired, Mortimer Grey lost everything – his reputation, probably most of his pension and of course a very well-paid job."

"Sounds like a good enough motive to me, sir!"

"It certainly does, Sergeant."

Sergeant O'Neil rang the doorbell. After a while, the door opened. The person who opened it was not quite what you would expect a butler to look like – even if he had been forced into early retirement a couple of months ago. Mortimer Grey had not shaved for days. He was wearing old tracksuit trousers and a dirty white vest. To make things worse, he smelled of alcohol. Only his formal and well-spoken manner reminded you that he had once been a butler:

run-down	herunterge-kommen
council house	Sozial-wohnung
shabby	schäbig
early retirement	Frührente
tracksuit trousers	Trainingshose
vest (GB)	Unterhemd
to stammer	stammeln, stottern
to observe	beobachten
steady	*hier*: ruhig
to dart	huschen

"How may I help you?" Mortimer Grey asked.
"I'm Inspector MacAlister from the Strathclyde Police and this is Sergeant O'Neil. May we come in for a moment?"
"May I ask why? Has something happened?"
"Grace Tate has been murdered."
"Good God!" exclaimed Mortimer Grey.
"May we come in?"
"Yes, of course," the butler **stammered**.

Not much later, Inspector MacAlister and Sergeant O'Neil were sitting opposite Mortimer Grey. All three of them had a cup of tea in front of them. The old butler took a sip of his. The inspector **observed** that his hand was **steady**. However, Mortimer Grey's eyes kept **darting** from him to the sergeant and back again.
"Do you recognize this?" asked the inspector, showing Mr Grey the handwritten note.
"I've never seen it before in my life," Mortimer Grey answered a little too fast.
"Georgina Tate said it was your handwriting," said the inspector.

Übung 7: Prepositions. Fügen Sie die richtigen Präpositionen ein!

under in at near

1. The letter was ______ the butler's handwriting.
2. Mortimer Grey did not live ______ the castle.
3. They all sat ______ the table drinking tea.
4. Mortimer Grey was ______ a lot of pressure.

despicable bunch	abscheulicher Haufen
matter-of-factly	nüchtern, sachlich
to leap	springen
to upset sth.	etw. umkippen, umwerfen
bin	Mülleimer
to grab	packen, greifen
wellingtons	Gummistiefel
sample	Probe, Muster
desperation	Verzweiflung
suspect	Verdächtiger
two-way mirror	Einwegspiegel
evidence	Beweis(e)
substantial	bedeutend, stichhaltig

"She would, wouldn't she? That woman just wants to see me ruined! If you ask me, one of the Tates murdered Grace. They are a **despicable bunch** if you want to know the truth!"

"Well, we did hear that you passed on inside information," the inspector said, **matter-of-factly**.

Mortimer Grey **leapt** to his feet, knocking his leg against the table and nearly **upsetting** his hot cup of tea.

"That was all a big misunderstanding!" he shouted.

"Please calm down, Mr Grey," Sergeant O'Neil said sternly.

Inspector MacAlister took out a pen and a piece of paper.

"If you would be so kind as to write your name down here?" he asked politely.

"Why should I? I told you I have nothing to do with this!"

Mortimer Grey suddenly ran towards the door, out of the living room and out of the house. Sergeant O'Neil went straight after him, catching up with him as the former butler was trying to hide behind a set of **bins**. Mortimer Grey saw him coming and threw a bin in his direction. The sergeant just managed to jump over it. Mortimer Grey tried to escape again, but Sergeant O'Neil **grabbed** him by his vest. "The butler did it!" he said triumphantly and took him back to the house.

Inspector MacAlister was waiting for them by the doorstep. He was holding the butler's green hunting jacket and **wellingtons** in his hands.

"I found these in the bathroom," he greeted the former butler, "and they are very wet. Do you have an explanation, Mr Grey?"
Mortimer Grey shook his head.
"I also found some shopping lists – very good writing **samples**. They match the writing on the note we found in Mrs Tate's pocket. Mortimer Grey, I arrest you for the murder of Grace Tate."
"No!" Mortimer Grey cried.
His cry echoed along the street and was full of **desperation**.

Übung 8: Synonyms. Lesen Sie weiter und setzen Sie die passenden Synonyme ein!

leapt | uneasily | explain to | directly

Soon after his arrest, Mortimer Grey sat **1.** nervously __________ in the interrogation room. Inspector MacAlister was looking the **suspect** **2.** straight __________ in the eye. Sergeant O'Neil was watching the interrogation from behind a **two-way mirror**.

"Do you want to **3.** tell __________ me what happened?" the inspector asked calmly. "The **evidence** against you is **substantial**."

The former butler **4.** jumped __________ to his feet and started to walk up and down nervously.

ϟ to catch sb.'s eye	jmd. auffallen
to wade	waten
current	Strömung

"I'm innocent, I swear!" Mortimer Grey exclaimed.

"So tell me what happened," Inspector MacAlister repeated himself.

"I wrote the note, I admit it. I also planned to meet up with Mrs Tate... I waited by the landing stage for over an hour, but she never came..."

"And why exactly did you want to meet her, Mr Grey?" asked the inspector.

"I really needed my job back," he replied. "I thought we could talk. I wanted to explain what had really happened. She had never listened to me before."

"How did your clothing get wet?" the inspector asked.

Mortimer Grey sighed. He was getting more nervous by the minute.[i] "You wouldn't believe me anyway!" he said angrily.

"I could try," replied the inspector.

by the minute = minütlich
minute by minute = Minute um Minute
by Monday = (spätestens) bis Montag
by now = inzwischen
by day = tagsüber

Mortimer Grey hesitated for a second. Then he said, "When she didn't come, I decided to walk back to my car..."

"What time was this?"

"It must have been around quarter past eight in the morning... My car was parked a little further down the loch... I like a good walk, you know? Anyway, suddenly something in the water **caught my eye**. I walked back to the shore and realized it was a body."

"What did you do then?" Inspector MacAlister asked calmly.

"I **waded** into the water and then I saw that it was Grace Tate. I panicked, ran to my car and drove off."

"Why didn't you call the police?"

“Isn’t it obvious?” Mortimer Grey asked agitatedly. “Look at the situation I’m in now!”
“Well, perhaps if you had contacted the police straight away, things might look better.”
Mortimer Grey sat down again. He put his head in his hands.
“It wasn’t me! I swear by God, I could never hurt a fly!”

Übung 9: Emphasis. Welches Wort hat die stärkere Bedeutung? Kreuzen Sie an!

1. ❒ swear ❒ promise
2. ❒ say ❒ cry
3. ❒ stunned ❒ surprised
4. ❒ nervous ❒ panicked
5. ❒ exclaim ❒ state

Inspector MacAlister and Sergeant O’Neil stood in front of the interrogation room.
“He should get an Oscar for best acting,” said the sergeant.
“Yes, he’s certainly good at drama,” stated the inspector. “But on the other hand, he has had a very hard time and now he’s our main murder suspect. If he’s innocent, the man must be close to a nervous breakdown.”
“How do you explain that nobody else found the body?”
“There are many possibilities. Maybe a **current** was responsible,

or the wind. Not to forget that nobody really searched the loch for her body."

"Well, **as far as I'm concerned**, you're too soft, sir."

"I just keep thinking about all the **quarrelling** going on in that family. There was something **guilty** in the air up at the castle, or something like that. I had the feeling that several of the Tates have something to hide."

Übung 10: Translation quiz. Übersetzen Sie und enträtseln Sie das Lösungswort!

1. furchtbar _ ☐ _ _ _
2. unschuldig _ _ _ _ _ ☐ _ _
3. schauspielern ☐ _ _
4. entlang _ ☐ _ _ _
5. Gummistiefel _ _ _ _ _ _ _ ☐ _ _ _
6. verfolgen _ ☐ _ _ _
7. genau (Adv.) _ _ _ _ _ _ ☐

Lösung: ☐☐☐☐☐☐☐

as far as I'm concerned	was mich betrifft
quarrelling	Streiten
guilty	schuldig
waste of time	Zeitverschwendung
to express	ausdrücken
doubt	Zweifel

"If you don't mind my saying so, sir, I think it's a **waste of time**. We've got our murderer."

"Yes, Sergeant, you may feel free to **express** your **doubt**. However, I say I return to Crowroad Castle for some further questioning. In the meantime, you do some further research[i] into the individual pasts of the family members. Try and find out who else could have had a reason to kill Grace Tate."

"You're the boss, sir!" replied the sergeant.

"Well observed, Sergeant," smiled Inspector MacAlister.

Im Englischen kann **research** sowohl als Nomen (Forschung) als auch als Verb **to research** (forschen) verwendet werden. Die Wendung „etwas erforschen" kann deshalb mit **to research into** oder auch als **to do research into** übersetzt werden.

4 Skeletons in the Closet

Just as Inspector MacAlister was putting his jacket on to return to Crowroad Castle, his office phone rang. It was Grace Tate's notary, Graham Bride. He wanted to talk to the inspector about a very important matter. Inspector MacAlister informed the sergeant that he was going to visit Graham Bride and made his way to the **posh** Glasgow district of Bearsden, where the notary was located.

Half an hour later the inspector entered a Victorian office building, which had the simple but **grand** aura of places like Number 10 Downing Street, where the British Prime Minister lived. A very serious-looking man in an even more serious-looking grey suit greeted the inspector with a **firm** handshake.

"Inspector MacAlister, very pleased to meet you. I'm Graham Bride, please take a seat," said the notary.

Inspector MacAlister sat down, his hand still **aching** slightly. Graham Bride was in every way a very large man – not someone you would like to fight with **in court**, the inspector thought.

posh	vornehm, schick
grand	erhaben
firm	fest
to ache	schmerzen
in court	vor Gericht
dreadful	schrecklich

"I'm glad you came," said the notary. "It's **dreadful**, just dreadful…," he continued, shaking his head sadly.

"Did you know Grace Tate well, Mr Bride?" the inspector wanted to know.

"Yes, I've known her for over twenty years. A great woman if you ask me, and that's something you can't say about most of them."
"Most of *them*?"
"Yes, the Tate family. Grace Tate held the family together. Without her I don't know what's going to happen."
"Could you tell me something about the **will**? Who is going to **gain** from it and who is anyone going to be disappointed?"

Übung 11: Odd one out. Welches Wort ist das „schwarze Schaf"?

1.	notary	lawyer	court	judge
2.	stylish	cheap	wealthy	posh
3.	shocking	dreadful	surprising	awful
4.	greeting	handshake	meeting	aching

The notary leant over his large, antique **oak** desk and looked the inspector straight in the eye. It was only now that MacAlister noticed that Graham Bride actually had a glass eye. This was a little confusing; the inspector had the feeling that the notary was looking at him and not looking at him at the same time.
"Today Grace Tate was found dead and we had an appointment this afternoon," Graham Bride said **conspiratorially**. "She wanted to **downgrade** James Tate in her will."
"And why?" asked the inspector.

will	Testament
to gain	gewinnen (an), profitieren
oak	Eiche
conspira-torially	verschwöre-risch
to downgrade	herabstufen, degradieren

"Because of that American **tart** he had married," the notary explained. "Mrs Tate considered the marriage to be scandalous."
"Because of the age difference?" the inspector asked.
"Yes," Graham Bride replied, "but there was also something else – something she did not tell me."
"How do you know?"
"Let's just say professional instinct."

> **Das Gerundium nach Verb + Präposition**
>
> Nach Verben, die mit einer Präposition verbunden sind, folgt immer die **ing**-Form, z. B.:
> to know about doing sth.
> to think of doing sth.
> to believe in doing sth.
> to dream of doing sth.
> to worry about doing sth.
> to be used to doing sth.

Graham Bride was so **convinced** of what he had just said, the inspector thought that he saw his glass eye **flash**.
"Did James Tate know about Grace Tate wanting (i) to downgrade him?"
The notary **shrugged**. "I'm not sure, I certainly didn't tell him. But maybe Grace did just to **annoy him**. It would certainly have been very like her."

ϟ tart	*hier*: Nutte, Schlampe
convinced	überzeugt
to flash	funkeln, blitzen
to shrug	die Achseln zucken
to annoy sb.	jmd. ärgern, nerven
ϟ good-for-nothing	Nichtsnutz
reluctantly	widerwillig, widerstrebend
impressive	beeindruckend

"What about the McPhersons?" Inspector MacAlister asked.
"Well, Grace Tate didn't like Daniel McPherson. However, she liked her daughter very much. She left quite a lot of money to her."
"Which would mean also to Daniel McPherson?"
"I assume so, Inspector," Graham Bride replied with a shrug, his glass eye flashing again. "Valeria is just blind with love for that **good-for-nothing**."

Übung 12: Translation. Lesen Sie weiter und fügen Sie die richtige Übersetzung ein!

The inspector stood up. Graham Bride's one good eye followed his **1.** Bewegungen ____________; his glass eye was still staring straight ahead.

"Well, thank you very much, Mr Bride," said the inspector. The notary **2.** stand auf ____________ and gave the inspector his hand. He **reluctantly** took it. Graham Bride gave it a good, strong shake.

"You have an... **impressive** **3.** Händedruck ____________ ____________," commented Inspector MacAlister.

"An old rugby **4.** Angewohnheit ____________, I'm afraid. That's also where I lost my eye. I could have been a professional player if that English idiot hadn't knocked it out," said the notary with a **5.** Seufzen ____________. "But that's life, isn't it: some you win, some you lose."

"I totally agree," answered the inspector, holding his aching hand for the second time that day.
He was suddenly glad that at school he had been no good at sport. I was obviously lucky to escape the rugby team, he thought to himself!

accusation	Anschuldigung
outrageous	unerhört
spark	Funke
to emphasize	betonen, deutlich machen
to down sth. in one	etw. auf ex trinken
to overhear	zufällig mithören
to suffer	leiden
to have a row	heftig streiten, Krach haben

It was already quite late in the evening by the time Inspector MacAlister eventually got to Crowroad Castle. He was standing in the drawing room again and had just mentioned the will to James Tate.
"These **accusations** are **outrageous**!" exclaimed James Tate.
He was standing with his back to the large drawing room fire, which was burning behind him. The bright **sparks** shooting out of the flames seemed to **emphasize** his anger. Inspector MacAlister and Sergeant O'Neil watched Joanne Tate give her husband a brandy. He **downed it in one**.
"I didn't even know she had downgraded me in the will!"
"You do go to the same exclusive gentlemen's club as her notary, Graham Bride. Maybe you **overheard** a conversation?" Inspector MacAlister suggested.
James Tate was about to explode when his wife suddenly said, "My husband never left the bedroom all night."
The inspector saw a look of slight surprise in James Tate's face.
"How do you know?" asked Sergeant O'Neil.
"I couldn't sleep most of the night. I lay awake reading a book or looking out of the window."
"Yes, yes, now I also remember," James supported her. "I woke up several times, too, and saw my wife awake every time."
"I see," Inspector MacAlister said sceptically.
"Why don't you go and interrogate Lara!" demanded Joanne suddenly. "As I told you before, I saw her walking past my window in the early hours of the morning."
"And what time was that?" the inspector wanted to know.
"I'm not sure, perhaps around seven," she replied.

"What motive would Lara have? As far as I can tell, she had a good relationship with her grandmother," the inspector said.
"Why don't you ask her about her ex-boyfriend who killed himself a year ago?" replied Joanne.
"Now, Joanne, I must say...," James interrupted.
He did not like these accusations against his daughter. However, his wife did not even let him finish his sentence.
"We all know Grace didn't think that boy was good enough for Lara. Grace forced them to separate. The poor young man just couldn't take it."

Übung 13: Adverbs. Wandeln Sie die Adjektive in Adverbien um!

1. slow ____________________
2. sceptical ____________________
3. fast ____________________
4. good ____________________

"Maybe you should try questioning my sister, Georgina," James Tate suddenly said, trying to change the subject. "She **suffered** the most under mother's dictatorship. Mother wouldn't even let Georgina go on holiday. You can ask who you want. They **had a row** about her holiday plans the evening before my mother's death. She wouldn't let Georgina go to Spain."
"I don't really think that's a reason to kill someone," replied the inspector. "I need to discuss the case with Sergeant O'Neil in private. Is there anywhere we could go?"
"Yes, the library is probably the best place," replied James Tate. "Please feel free to use it, Inspector."

5 The Secret of Crowroad Castle

Inspector MacAlister and Sergeant O'Neil sat in the castle's library. As far as the eye could see, there were books neatly stored in the high wooden shelves that almost touched the ceiling. The policemen had retreated to this quiet room to discuss the case in private.

neatly stored	sauber aufgeräumt
to retreat	sich zurückziehen
to sway	sich wiegen, schwanken
suspicious	verdächtig
bolt of lightning	Blitz

"The more we look into this case, the more people we find who had a reason to kill Grace Tate," said the inspector with a sigh.

It started to rain heavily outside. A tree, swaying in the wind, kept knocking against the large library window.

"I still believe Mortimer Grey did it," said the sergeant. "I mean, rich families are always arguing over money and hiding dark secrets from each other. But it doesn't automatically have to lead to murder."

"But in some cases it does," the inspector pointed out. "Did you manage to find out anything else about Joanne Tate? The notary said that there might be something else as well as the obvious age difference."

"Yes, I remember. But it seems there is nothing suspicious about her – except perhaps her enormously high high-heels," he grinned. Suddenly a noise came from the back of the library. It sounded like a book had fallen off the shelves. At the same time a bolt of lightning shot across the dark autumn sky.

Übung 14: Translation. Übersetzen Sie die Begriffe ins Englische!

1. Streiten ______________________
2. sich zurückziehen ______________________
3. verdächtig ______________________
4. offensichtlich ______________________

"Is there anybody there?" asked the inspector.

There was no answer. The two policemen stood up and walked in the direction of where the noise had come from. All of a sudden some heavy and large books came crashing down on top of them. Inspector MacAlister and Sergeant O'Neil just managed to jump to the side. The sound of running footsteps echoed through the library,(i) only to be interrupted by another loud clap of thunder from outside. They ran after the person who had obviously wanted to hurt them. Sergeant O'Neil was faster than his superior. He saw what he thought was long blonde hair disappear behind one of the shelves(i) at the very end of the library. He ran faster and was convinced that he was close to

Pluralbildung

Endet das Substantiv auf einen Konsonanten und **-y**, so wird das **-y** im Plural zu **-ies**, z. B. library - libraries. Endet das Substantiv auf **-f** oder **-fe**, so wird **-f/-fe** normalerweise durch **-ves** ersetzt, z. B.: shelf - shelves. Daneben gibt es zahlreiche unregelmäßige Pluralfomen, z. B. man - men, foot - feet.

catching up with the person. The sergeant reached the end of the library, but the person was gone – as if they had **disappeared into thin air**. Quite out of breath, Inspector MacAlister eventually caught up with the sergeant.

"Where did he go?" the inspector **panted**.

"I think it was a she," the sergeant corrected him. "I saw long blonde hair."

"So where did she go?"

Sergeant O'Neil shrugged his shoulders. "I have no idea! Can people run through walls?"

Inspector MacAlister inspected the wall closely.

"Maybe there's a secret passage," he said. "There must be a button or something somewhere."

However, they could not find anything.

"Wherever it is, it's damn well hidden!" the inspector remarked. "You said she had long blonde hair?"

The sergeant nodded.

Inspector MacAlister sighed. "That's not really a great help. Valeria, Lara, Joanne and even Georgina Tate all have long blonde hair."

ϟ to disappear into thin air	sich in Luft auflösen
to pant	keuchen
to rip sth. off	etwas ab-, wegreißen
fashionable	in Mode, modisch
to head for	*hier*: zusteuern auf
garment	Kleidungsstück

At that moment the inspector's mobile phone rang. It was the coroner.

While the inspector talked to him, the sergeant continued to try and find the entrance to the secret passage.

"That was Miles," Inspector MacAlister said after finishing the call. "He told me that he found a button in Grace Tate's hand. It must have been the last thing she held on to. The coroner said she may have **ripped it off** before she fell dead into the loch."

"Does it belong to a green hunting jacket?" asked the sergeant, thinking of Mortimer Grey's wet jacket they had found.

> Es gibt zahlreiche Phrasal Verbs mit **hold**.
>
> Einige Beispiele:
> to hold on = sich festhalten; durchhalten
> to hold on to sth. = (sich an) etw. festhalten, etw. behalten
> to hold back = verbergen; zurückhalten
> to hold in = zügeln, zurückhalten
> to hold out = reichen; durchhalten
> to hold up = hochhalten; aufhalten

"No, it's a silvery, shiny button. More likely it belongs to one of these women's silver or gold tops which are quite **fashionable** just now."

"Wait a minute...," said Sergeant O'Neil.

"That's exactly what I'm thinking," the inspector replied. "Joanne Tate was wearing one of those tops on the day they arrived. I remember seeing it when we went through the digital photographs yesterday that Lara Tate had taken of the family meeting."

Inspector MacAlister and Sergeant O'Neil turned and **headed** straight **for** Joanne Tate's castle bedroom.

"What the hell do you think you're doing?" demanded Joanne Tate angrily when she discovered the policemen in her room.

But they didn't answer and all she could do was just stand and watch them search through her wardrobe. At last Sergeant O'Neil found the **garment** they were looking for.

"We were looking for this!" the sergeant said triumphantly.

"Are you thinking about changing your style?" Joanne Tate asked rudely.

The sergeant ignored her and handed the top to Inspector MacAlister, who examined it.

"No button missing," he said.

"Oh, I'm the main murder suspect now, or what!?" exclaimed Joanne Tate. "Well, if that's your clue, why not try Lara's wardrobe? She's got exactly the same top!"

Übung 15: Unscramble. Lesen Sie weiter und ordnen Sie die Buchstaben zu einem sinnvollen Wort!

Accompanied by shouts of **1.** testorp ________________, the policemen also searched Lara's wardrobe. **Word had spread** very fast in the **2.** lsacte ________________ and the Tates were all standing in front of Lara's room, trying to see what was going on. It did not take the **3.** pnamecilo ________________ long to find what they were looking for: Lara Tate's top had a button missing. Sergeant O'Neil **sniffed** at the **4.** tgarmen ________________. It had also been freshly washed.

"I loved my grandmother. I would never have killed her!" exclaimed Lara after the inspector had stated his suspicions.

"And what about your ex-boyfriend? We heard you loved him very much, too?" Inspector MacAlister asked.

"It was sad he killed himself, but grandmother was right – he was not the right person for me," she replied coldly.

"My God, you are becoming more and more like her every day!" James Tate said, shaking his head.

"Shut up, Daddy!" shouted Lara.

"I'm afraid I'll have to **take you in** for questioning," Inspector MacAlister said.

He noticed Joanne Tate grinning **wickedly** at her stepdaughter.

Lara Tate glowered back.
"So she's got you wrapped around her little finger, hasn't she?" Lara Tate spat at her father.
"Were you in the library earlier on?" the inspector asked.
Lara did not answer.
"While you were consulting with Sergeant O'Neil in the library, we were all having tea together," said Georgina, trying to support her niece. "Lara was with us, too."
"Yes, but she left for a while to go to the toilet, don't you remember?" Joanne reminded her.
Lara Tate wanted to jump at her stepmother. She was wild with anger. Sergeant O'Neil could just hold her back in time. She struggled to get herself free, but eventually she calmed down a little.
"Okay, I admit it. I was in the library. But I just wanted to hear how things were going with the investigation."
"And the books?" asked the inspector.
"That was an accident, I swear!"
"I'm afraid that's not good enough. We'll have to take you in."
"But… you can't… Daddy, do something!" cried Lara.
James just looked away. He could not bear to look his terrified daughter in the eye.

to accompany	begleiten
word had spread	es hatte sich herumgesprochen
to sniff at sth.	an etw. riechen
⚡ take sb. in	jmd. festnehmen
wickedly	boshaft
to glower	finster blicken
to wrap around	wickeln um
to spit	*hier*: fauchen
niece	Nichte
investigation	Ermittlung, Untersuchung
to bear sth.	*hier*: etw. ertragen
terrified	entsetzt

Just as the policemen were taking Lara Tate to the car, Sergeant O'Neil received a call from Constable Roy, who was carrying out further research into the family members' past. While the sergeant was talking, Inspector MacAlister put Lara into the backseat of the car. After Sergeant O'Neil had finished the call, he hurried over to the inspector.

"I think we may have been a little hasty," he said.

"Why is that, Sergeant?" [i]

"There appears to be something **fishy** about Joanne Tate's past after all. She has not been quite honest about it."

Sergeant O'Neil hesitated.

"Yes?" the inspector **encouraged** him to continue.

The sergeant cleared his throat.

"Well, Joanne Fraser, as her **maiden name** is, used to be an English high class call girl. Probably Grace Tate found out about her past..."

> Titel wie **Inspector** und **Sergeant** werden im Englischen groß geschrieben, wenn es sich um eine direkte Anrede innerhalb der wörtlichen Rede handelt oder sie als Teil eines Namens verwendet werden, z. B. Inspector Davies. In allen anderen Fällen werden diese Titel und Berufsbezeichnungen klein geschrieben, z. B. The sergeant hesitated.

"I see," said the inspector thoughtfully, looking over at Lara. "Can you hand me that piece of clothing?"

Sergeant O'Neil gave him the top that he was still holding in his hand. The inspector looked at the place where the label usually is. It had been cut out. He walked over to the car and asked Lara to try it on. As he had guessed: it was too big. After Lara had taken the top off again, Inspector MacAlister told Sergeant O'Neil to wait by the car and then he hurried back to the castle.

It did not take the inspector long to find Joanne. She was up in her bedroom.

"Would you kindly try this top on for me, Mrs Tate?" he said and held up the top.

"Why should I!"

"Because I think it belongs to you."

At that moment James Tate entered the bedroom.

Übung 16: Reading comprehension. Beantworten Sie die Fragen zum Text in ganzen Sätzen!

1. What did Lara Tate think about her grandmother's opinion of her boyfriend?

2. What does James Tate think about his daughter?

3. Why did Lara Tate get very angry with her stepmother?

4. What did Joanne Tate used to be?

"What's going on here?" James Tate asked.

"I believe your wife killed your mother, Mr Tate."

"Nonsense!" spat Joanne Tate. "I have an alibi!"

"Does she?" Inspector MacAlister asked, looking at James Tate.

"Yes, she was with me every minute."

Inspector MacAlister showed him the top.

"This actually does not fit your daughter, Mr Tate, but I truly believe it would fit your wife."

ϟ fishy	verdächtig
to encourage	ermutigen
maiden name	Mädchenname

With a sigh, James Tate gave in. "To be honest, I woke up in the morning and she was gone. I didn't say anything because she gave me an alibi, but now that the evidence..."

"Shut up, you fool!" Joanne Tate shouted.

Her American accent **slipped**. Joanne Tate suddenly sounded English.

By now James Tate looked really confused.

"Now would you kindly try this on?" said the inspector waving the top in her direction. "I believe you **swapped** yours with Lara's."

Joanne sat down on the bed.

"Oh hell!" she **cursed** in the broadest English accent. "I don't need to – you're right. Grace had found out about my past as a call girl..."

"As a what?" James Tate exclaimed.

"...She was **blackmailing me**: Either I **divorced** James or she would tell him... During the night I couldn't sleep. I saw her passing my window in the early hours of the morning... I followed her and..."

"Joanne!" exclaimed James. His legs nearly **gave way**.

"Yes, I hit her over the head with the next best branch I could find!" **hissed** Joanne Tate.

Inspector MacAlister helped her to her feet and took her to the police car. As they drove off, what was left of the Tate family stood in silence on the castle stairs and watched the car disappear down the drive.

to slip	*hier*: entgleiten, nachlassen
to swap	tauschen
to curse	fluchen
to blackmail sb.	jmd. erpressen
to divorce	sich scheiden lassen
to give way	nachgeben, einknicken
to hiss	zischen, fauchen

A Bullet to the Brain

Oliver Astley

1 Death to the King

The news came one Saturday morning from a young woman who sounded very upset and spoke with a strong foreign accent.

"Yes, hello, police? You must come. He is dead! His skin is cold and there is blood all over the floor. You must come here as soon as possible, please!"

Chief Inspector Evans had just arrived at the office and was listening to a **recording** of the telephone call. There was always a lot of crime in London on a Friday night, but he was not prepared for what he was about to hear.

The **operator** was very calm and asked for the woman's name and location. She was calling from a mobile phone.

"My name is Helena Kowalska. I have just come to work… I am the cleaner at a nightclub called 'Lust' in Charing Cross. I am sorry, but my English is not very good. When will you be here?"

"We'll send someone over as soon as we can, Mrs Kowalska," the operator replied. "Please stay where you are and let me take some more information. Do you know who the dead person is?"

"Of course!" she **exclaimed**. "It is the big boss. He has shot himself. The gun is still in his hand."

Inspector Evans could not believe his ears.

"The big boss?" he repeated to everyone in the room after the recording had ended. "Does that mean what I think it means?"

recording	Aufnahme
operator	Telefonist
to exclaim	ausrufen

Some people were nodding their heads in answer to the inspector's question; others **shrugged** unknowingly. Could Stanley Cooper really be dead?

Stanley Cooper was not only the owner of Lust, but a **notorious crime lord** who ran a large chain of bars and nightclubs in London's West End. He also owned a **dog track** in Walthamstow. The Metropolitan Police called him the "King of the Underworld" because they believed that he and his gangsters were responsible for much of the **violence** in the area. Unfortunately for them, they had no **solid proof**.

to shrug	die Achseln zucken
notorious	berüchtigt
crime lord	Verbrecherkönig
dog track	Hunderennbahn
violence	Gewalt
solid proof	eindeutige Beweise
forensics	Spurensicherung
crime scene	Tatort
in charge of	zuständig für
to growl	brummen
suspicious	verdächtig
Don't leave any stone unturned.	Lasst nichts unversucht!

"The call came in less than twenty minutes ago," said a deep female voice. "The **forensics** team are already on their way to examine the **crime scene**. Evans, you should go and join them. Something tells me that Cooper didn't kill himself, and if I'm right, this is going to be your case."

It was Superintendent Fisher, the officer **in charge of** the station. She was a very powerful woman. Everything she said sounded like an order.

"Yes, ma'am," replied Inspector Evans. "I'll take Sandra with me, if that's okay. We've both been working on cases involving Cooper's gang lately."

"That was going to be my next suggestion," the superintendent **growled**. "I want you to treat this death as **suspicious** from the start. **Don't leave any stone unturned** when you're down there."

"Of course not, ma'am."

"Where is Checchino, anyway? It's not like her to be late. Find her and get going!"
"Right away, ma'am," the inspector said and left the room.

Übung 1: Multiple choice. Welcher Satz ist korrekt? Kreuzen Sie an!

1. a) ☐ The cleaner has a strong foriegn accent.
   b) ☐ The cleaner has a strong foreign accent.

2. a) ☐ The inspector could not believe his ears.
   b) ☐ The inspector could not belief his ears.

3. a) ☐ You must treat this death as suspicious.
   b) ☐ You must treat this dead as suspicious.

4. a) ☐ It looks like Stanley Cooper has shoot himself.
   b) ☐ It looks like Stanley Cooper has shot himself.

Inspector Sandra Checchino was sitting in the staff kitchen when Inspector Evans **burst into** the room.
"Ah, Sandra, there you are!" he called.
She looked up from her large cup of coffee in surprise.
"Oh, it looks like someone had a long night last night!" he said in a friendly tone.
Inspector Checchino smiled weakly.

"Yes, you could say that, Gary. I just haven't had time to put on any make-up."
"Never mind, you look no worse without it," he joked. "Anyway, you've just missed some important news. You'll never believe what happened last night!"
Inspector Checchino waited for him to continue.
"We've got to go and see our friend Stanley Cooper!" he said.
"Oh, no, not again!" she **groaned** and looked back down at her coffee. "That man never cooperates. He won't tell us anything. What have he and his **thugs** done this time?"
"That's what we have to find out," he replied mysteriously. "But you are right about one thing: Cooper definitely won't be telling us anything today, that's for sure. He's been found dead in his office at Lust. It looks like **suicide**."
Inspector Checchino opened her eyes wide.
"Mamma mia!" she said in a parody of her Italian relatives. "Stanley Cooper's dead? We should get going right away."
She quickly drank what was left of her coffee, which was still rather hot, and walked out of the kitchen with Inspector Evans.

to burst into	hineinstürzen
to groan	stöhnen
thug	Schläger(typ)
suicide	Selbstmord
elaborate	kunstvoll

The nightclub looked like a small building from the outside. The entrance was between two bars on a narrow side street off Charing Cross Road. Large, colourful posters on the door advertised which disc jockeys were playing on which nights, and red neon lights above the door spelt out in **elaborate** letters the word "Lust".
"This would be a nice place for a first date," Inspector Evans said, smiling at Inspector Checchino. "Look, we missed DJs Mad Daddy and Divine Lickz last night!"

"You and your jokes," she replied **flatly**. "I think we're both a bit too old for places like these, don't you?"
"I certainly am," he said, "but you're still young, free and single, Sandra. You'd quickly find yourself a date in a place like this."
"Don't make me laugh. I'm thirty-five next month. And we meet enough thugs at work – I don't want to date one as well."
"Lust is very exclusive," said Inspector Evans. "Well, it is if you compare it to Cooper's other bars, at least…"
The uniformed policeman who was guarding the entrance smiled and let the pair inside. They walked down the stairs and passed straight through the **cloakroom** into the bar area. The air was heavy with the smell of alcohol, and the floor was **littered with** empty bottles and cigarette stubs. It was quite **sticky** underfoot.
The large, pink leather sofas against the walls looked very out of place in the daylight that shone through the tall windows.

flatly	ausdruckslos
cloakroom	Garderobe
littered with	übersät mit
sticky	klebrig
investigator	Ermittler(in)
dread	Grauen
ϟ to snuff it	draufgehen, abkratzen
solemnly	düster, ernst
chest	Brust

"Nice décor," Inspector Checchino whispered sarcastically.
A young woman wearing jeans and a jumper was sitting on one of the silver and red bar stools. She did not notice the two police officers entering the room because she was busy talking on her mobile phone in a loud voice.
"That must be the cleaner," said Inspector Evans, who spoke a few words of Polish. "We'll talk to her later. Come on, let's go and see our man."
Although she was an experienced **investigator**, Inspector Checchino always felt a sense of **dread** before seeing dead bodies, and today was no exception. Her colleague, on the other hand, seemed to be nothing but happy about Stanley Cooper's death.

Übung 2: Synonyms. Welche Wörter gehören zusammen? Ordnen Sie zu!

1. ☐	dread	**a)** family
2. ☐	flatly	**b)** artistic
3. ☐	relatives	**c)** expressionlessly
4. ☐	elaborate	**d)** fear

The forensics team were busy taking photographs when Inspectors Evans and Checchino entered the office.
"It's really true, then, the King has **snuffed it**?" Inspector Evans asked everyone in the room.
Near the back of the office, a man's head appeared from behind the desk and grinned.
"A single shot to the brain," he said as he stood up.
It was Vash Singh, one of the forensics experts. His thick glasses made his eyes look as large as saucers.
"There's no sign of a struggle at all," he said. "Just look around this room; you can see for yourselves how tidy it is."
The office looked completely normal apart from the two legs that were sticking out from behind the desk. Inspector Evans walked up to look at the rest of the body.
"Hmm, it's certainly less tidy at this end of the room, that's for sure," he said **solemnly**.
Stanley Cooper's body was lying face up in a pool of blood. His mouth was open and his arms were resting on either side of his fat **chest**.

The inspector's eyes moved directly to the gun in the man's[i] left hand. "So, what do you think, Vash? Is it really possible that he shot himself?"

"I'd say so, Gary," he replied. "It does look like suicide, but we still can't **rule out** murder. There'll have to be a full ballistic analysis. We can only guess the facts until then."

Im Englischen steht bei Personen und Tieren üblicherweise der **s**-Genitiv, bei Dingen der **of**-Genitiv. Der Genitiv drückt Besitzverhältnisse oder Zugehörigkeiten aus oder gibt die Urheberschaft an.

"Does it look like the body's been moved at all?"

Vash shook his head.

"There's a lot of blood here, but it's all in one place," he said.

Inspector Checchino walked over from the doorway and looked at the body. The dead man had short, grey hair and a big **moustache** that sat above his top lip like a lazy **caterpillar**. Even dead, he still has the same arrogant expression on his face, she thought.

"Do you have any idea when this happened?" she asked.

Vash pushed his glasses up his nose and explained that the body had already been a little **stiff** when they had arrived just after ten o'clock. They had also measured the temperature.

"I'd say he died between 5 a.m. and 6 a.m.," he **concluded**.

"And you've found nothing unusual at all?" she continued.

Vash shrugged.

"I wouldn't expect his arms to be in that position if he shot himself," he said, "but on the other hand, it's not impossible."

to rule out	ausschließen
moustache	Schnurrbart
caterpillar	Raupe
stiff	steif
to conclude	*hier*: schlussfolgern
to bring to justice	zur Rechenschaft ziehen
collar	Kragen
evidence	Beweis(e)
security camera footage	Aufnahmen der Überwachungskameras

"Well you've been trying to bring this man to justice for a long time, Sandra," said Inspector Evans. "It looks to me like someone may have helped you out."
"Maybe," she said quietly, staring at the dead man's arms.
Then one of the other forensic experts said that there was something interesting about Cooper's shirt: she had noticed a small amount of lipstick on the collar when she was taking photographs of the body.

Übung 3: Prepositions. Lesen Sie weiter und unterstreichen Sie die richtige Präposition!

Inspector Checchino was examining a computer monitor **1.** at / in the corner of the office. It showed sixteen small pictures **2.** of / from the main rooms in the nightclub **3.** in / from different angles, including the office they were standing in. It also showed two more pictures **4.** of / over the street outside.

"There should be a lot of evidence on this, Gary," she said, pointing **5.** on / at the security camera footage.

Inspector Evans looked at the screen and scratched his head.

"Hmm," he replied slowly. "There might have been if someone hadn't switched it **6.** off / of. Look, it's not recording."

2 Find the Woman

"Sorry to keep you waiting, Mrs Kowalska," Inspector Evans began. "Could you begin by telling us what the nightclub was like when you came to work this morning?"

"Everything looked normal," she replied, looking him in the eye. "The doors were locked, and the lights were off. The sign outside was still turned on, but that happens quite often."

"Is there an alarm system **fitted** here?" he asked.

Inspector Checchino was noting down the information and looked up at the cleaner when she did not reply.

"Do you have an alarm?" the inspector repeated.

"Yes. Sorry, I do not understand everything you say," Helena said. "The alarm was turned off when I arrived. I thought that the big boss was here, or the manager. They sometimes stay in the office and play poker until the morning."

"I see. Can you tell me the manager's name, please?"

"Omar Omari," the cleaner smiled. "He is such a charming man, Inspector. He is always very friendly to me."

to fit sth.	etw. einbauen
to sigh	seufzen
rumour	Gerücht

"How many other people work here at the club?"

"I am not sure. I do not know most of them personally," Helena replied slowly. "There is a list of names and telephone numbers on the notice board. I can give you a copy."

"That would be very helpful, thank you," he said. "It would also help

us a great deal if you could answer a few more questions."
The cleaner **sighed** a little and looked at her watch.
"I must do some work," she complained. "I have two more places to go to this morning."
"I'll try to be brief, Mrs Kowalska. Have you heard of any arguments involving Stanley Cooper recently?"
The young lady shook her head.
"I do not see the big boss often. And when I do, he does not tell me anything like that," she explained.
"I see," the inspector said, "but maybe you've heard other people talking about him?"
"You should talk to Omar," she replied. "He knows much more about his private life. In fact, he sometimes complains that he is too – hmm, what is the word? – too involved in it."
Inspector Evans paused and looked across at his colleague.
"I didn't necessarily mean his private life, Mrs Kowalska. Do you know anything about any business deals, for example, or have you heard any **rumours** involving other gangs?"
"Gangs?" she repeated, shocked. "Oh no! I am sorry, I really have nothing to do with any of that. I am just the cleaner here."

Übung 4: Unscramble. Bringen Sie die Buchstaben in die richtige Reihenfolge!

1. sumurro ____________________
2. crenyelt ____________________
3. locarl ____________________
4. launusu ____________________

The police had been knocking for five minutes when Omar Omari finally opened the front door to his apartment in North London. His wild, curly hair was hanging over his eyes, and he was only half dressed. He did not seem at all surprised by the news of his boss's death.

⚡ **swine**	Schweinehund
He had that coming.	Das hat er verdient.
sternly	streng
exaggerated	übertrieben
stain	Fleck
to suppose	annehmen, vermuten

"So the dirty old **swine** is dead?" he laughed. "**He had that coming.**"

"Please take this seriously, Mr Omari," Inspector Checchino said **sternly**. "We're talking about a man's life – and possibly a very serious crime."

"What do you mean by 'possibly'?" he asked.

"We're still trying to find out exactly what happened last night," she said calmly. "May we come inside?"

"Why, of course. Do come on in, Officers," the man said with **exaggerated** politeness. "Take a seat in the lounge and I'll be right with you."

The pair sat down on an old, blue futon that was covered in large **stains**.

Omar came back a minute later wearing a white T-shirt. He was also carrying a rolled-up pair of socks which he put on as the police began their interview.

"Could you begin by telling us when you left work last night, Mr Omari?" Inspector Checchino asked in a tolerant voice.

"Yeah, it was a really busy night and I stayed until the end. We had some great DJs playing – Mad Daddy was there, you know – so it was an important event for us all. It went really well."

He brushed his hair away from his eyes and looked at the two inspectors, who both seemed to be expecting him to say more.

"Oh, I was there until about 4:30, I **suppose**," he finally answered.

Inspector Checchino wrote down the information.
"Did anybody see you leave?" she asked.
"At that time in the morning? No. At least, nobody I know. I got the night bus back up here."
"Hmm. Well, what can you tell us about Stanley Cooper – was he alone when you left the club?"
"No. A man called Bruno Tartufo was in the office with him all night," he explained. "He's the boss's right-hand man. They're almost always together, and he was still there when I left."
"And apart from yourself, Mr Omari, how many people have **access** to Mr Cooper's office?" Inspector Checchino asked.
Omar did not **flinch**.

access	Zugang
to flinch	zusammen-zucken
expressionlessly	ausdruckslos
to wrap around	wickeln um
⚡ fruity	verrückt, flott
to pour sb. sth.	jmd. etw. einschenken

"I only go in there when I'm invited. Normally I work in my own office across the hall, but I know some people who don't have to wait for an invitation, if you know what I mean."
The young man grinned at the two inspectors with perfect white teeth. They looked back at him **expressionlessly**, not understanding what was so amusing.
"Well, it's what they always say at the start of a police investigation, isn't it? Cherchez la femme! And I can tell you right away that Cooper had a young lady friend: a Miss Kim Watt. She had him **wrapped around** her little finger.
"Kim Watt?" repeated Inspector Checchino.
"Yes, Kim Watt the Kumquat, I call her – a **fruity** little thing. She manages Cooper's dog track in Walthamstow. But I've seen her in Lust quite a lot lately, too. She always comes to the bar as soon as she arrives and **pours** herself a gin and tonic, the little madam."
"Did you see her at the club last night?"

Omar shook his head and brushed back his hair again.

"Who else would Mr Cooper let into his office?" asked the inspector, who suddenly felt there was something strangely attractive about the club manager.

henchman	Scherge, Handlanger
faithful	treu
to wonder	sich fragen
to blink	blinzeln
sensible	vernünftig
to commit a crime	ein Verbrechen begehen
like Fort Knox	wie eine Festung

"Just his idiot **henchmen**, I guess. They do everything for Cooper, and they have keys to all of his bars and clubs. **Faithful** as dogs, they are, and just as stupid."

Inspector Evans laughed a little and took down the men's names.

"Now then," he continued, "has anything happened lately that could have made Stanley Cooper someone's enemy?"

"Lots!" Omar exclaimed. "And you're asking the right person, let me tell you! He tried to get me involved in some of his 'business activities' outside the nightclub, but I didn't want to have anything to do with it."

"Is that what Helena Kowalska meant when she said that you knew about his private life?" Inspector Checchino **wondered** aloud.

"Ah, Helena," sighed Omar. "She doesn't know the half of it. But yes, I've told her some things in private. The boss wanted me to 'take a message to a client' in Walthamstow. I'm not paid to go on dangerous missions like that, though!"

Das englische **in private** bedeutet zumeist nicht „privat", sondern vielmehr „vertraulich, unter vier Augen". Als Adverb wird „privat" zumeist mit **privately** oder auch **personally** übersetzt.

"One last thing, Mr Omari," said Inspector Evans towards the end of the interview. "Do you know how to operate the security camera system at Lust?"

"Of course," he replied. "I'm the manager there, aren't I? Actually,

I don't have to do very much at all. It runs automatically, you see. The cameras are connected to a computer that saves the videos for a month, and then they're deleted."
"Someone stopped the computer from recording last night," the inspector explained. "Have you any idea who that might have been?"
Omar **blinked** at him.
"No. But it seems like a **sensible** thing to do if you're going to **commit a crime**, doesn't it?" he said dryly.
"Is it possible that there's another copy of the videos somewhere?" Inspector Evans continued. "For example, is the footage sent to another company, or to Mr Cooper's home computer?"
"Nope," said Omar simply. "His house is the one place that is totally secure. Bad Manor Park. I've heard that it's **like Fort Knox** there!"

Übung 5: Short Answers. Beantworten Sie die folgenden Fragen in der Kurzform!

1. Does Helena Kowalska like the club manager?

   ____

2. Did Stanley Cooper talk a lot with the cleaner at Lust?

   ____

3. Was Omar Omari wearing trousers when he opened the door?

   ____

4. Is there a second copy of the security camera footage?

   ____

"Bruno Tartufo!" repeated Inspector Evans after they left the apartment. "This isn't the first time we've heard that name lately."
The Metropolitan Police were trying to fight the sale of cocaine in and around the West End, and several unimportant members of a drugs ring had mentioned Tartufo.
"Another fine Italian citizen in the city of London," said Inspector Checchino ironically. "We're not related, before you say anything."
Inspector Evans was more interested in finding Tartufo than making jokes. He **radioed** the station.
"I need addresses for Bruno Tartufo and Kim Watt," he said. "And make sure that the **family liaison officer** reaches Stanley Cooper's daughter before the Polish cleaner starts to **gossip**!"

to radio	(an)funken
family liaison officer	Opferschutz-beamter
to gossip	tratschen
marble	Marmor
intercom	Gegensprech-anlage
seductive	verführerisch
redhead	Rothaarige

Later that day, towards the mid-afternoon, the two detectives drove to an elegant town house in Chelsea. It was the address of the third and last Kim Watt in central London. The first two had said that they did not know anything about anyone called Stanley Cooper.
The pair had also tried to speak to Bruno Tartufo, but there was nobody home.
Inspector Evans walked up the three white **marble** steps leading to the large, black front door, rang the bell and waited.
The voice that eventually came through the **intercom** was as sweet as honey.
"Hello?" she asked, her voice almost **seductive**. "Who's there?"
"Police, ma'am," replied the inspector with a small smile. "Please open up!"
The first thing the police saw on the other side of the door was a tall **redhead** with a surprised expression on her face. Her lips were

painted bright red. Moments later, a short man with a thin moustache entered the hallway and stood next to her. He looked at the police and put his arm around the woman.

unmistakably	unverwechselbar
to hiss	zischen, fauchen

"Miss Watt?" Inspector Evans began.
"Yes?"
"We've come to talk to you about Stanley Cooper. May we come inside for a moment?"
"Hah! You've caught him at last, have you?" joked the small man in an **unmistakably** Italian accent.
"Bruno, be quiet!" Kim **hissed**.
"Ah, and you must be Mr Tartufo!" the inspector smiled. "We have a lot to discuss."

Übung 6: Odd one out. Welches Wort ist das „schwarze Schaf"? Unterstreichen Sie!

1. recording footage access
2. evidence rumour gossip
3. struggle fight guard
4. hiss stain groan

3 A Headless Organisation

After over an hour of interviews, Inspectors Evans and Checchino left Kim Watt's house in Chelsea and set off back to the station. They talked about their **impressions** on the way.

"I never thought the notorious Bruno Tartufo would be such a short man!" began Inspector Evans. "Even you're taller than him, Sandra!"

She gave a little laugh but kept her eyes fixed on the road.

impression	Eindruck
Don't be fooled.	Lass dich nicht täuschen.
to intimidate	einschüchtern
to prove	beweisen

"**Don't be fooled**," she said, "small people can be dangerous."

"I didn't like the way he was staring at Kim whenever she spoke," her colleague continued. "He was **intimidating** her. Do you think she was telling the truth?"

"People like her are never honest about everything, Gary," she replied, "but she did take the news about Cooper very badly."

"For a few moments, maybe, then she was perfectly normal again. I know she says she was at the dog track in Walthamstow all evening, but that closed just after midnight, and she has no alibi for the time of the shooting."

"Not many people will have an alibi that they can **prove**, Gary. After all, it was between five and six o'clock in the morning. I'm sure that you and I were asleep like most other people in London, but nobody can prove that either, can they?"

Das Wort **news** ist trotz des **-s** am Wortende eines der englischen Substantive, die nie im Plural, sondern immer im Singular stehen. Es erscheint also stets mit der Singularform des Verbs und nie mit dem unbestimmten Artikel: **That's good news.** – Das sind gute Nachrichten!

Zudem bezieht sich **news** nur auf veröffentlichte Nachrichten(sendungen) oder Neuigkeiten. Eine (private) Benachrichtigung wird dagegen als **message** übersetzt.

Inspector Evans turned to his colleague and grinned.
"Only because you've **turned me down** so often, Sandra," he said. "I know better than to ask you out on a Friday night now."
Inspector Checchino laughed in amusement.
"Oh, **come off it!** You're a good friend, but we tried that once, if you remember. It would never work."
"I know, I know," he said. "You can't **blame me for** trying, though."
There was a short pause in the conversation.
"What about Bruno?" he asked.
Inspector Checchino **frowned**.
"Hmm, yes, what about him?" she agreed. "He didn't appear at all shocked by the news.[i] And I find it very suspicious that he says he left the nightclub at exactly 5 a.m., don't you?"
The car came to a halt at some red traffic lights and she looked Inspector Evans in the eye.
"Moments before Cooper was killed," he agreed, scratching his chin. "But Bruno says that his boss was expecting a visitor and that he wanted to be alone when that person arrived. That's why he left the club at that time."
"So he says, yes," sighed Inspector Checchino. "I don't believe that story for a second. It's very **convenient** for Bruno, isn't it?"

to turn sb. down	jmd. einen Korb geben
⚡ Come off it!	Ach was! / Red doch keinen Unsinn!
to blame sb. for sth.	*hier*: jmd. etw. verübeln
to frown	die Stirn runzeln
convenient	günstig, passend

Inspector Evans nodded slowly.
"It is, yes. But it could be convenient for us that we found him at Kim Watt's house today. According to Omar, she was going out with Cooper, wasn't she? So, what do you think she was doing with Bruno on a Saturday afternoon?"

Übung 7: Opposites quiz. Finden Sie das Gegenteil der folgenden Wörter und enträtseln Sie das Lösungswort!

1. turn down ☐ _ _ _ _ _
2. unfaithful _ _ _ _ _ _ _ ☐
3. depart _ _ _ ☐ _ _
4. excited ☐ _ _ _ _
5. frown _ _ ☐ _ _

Lösung: ☐ ☐ ☐ ☐ ☐

Back at the police station, the two detectives met Superintendent Fisher to discuss their findings. She listened to everything they had to say, but she was not interested in the smaller details: her favourite football club Arsenal was playing at 5:30 p.m., and she was planning to watch the game from start to finish.
"Let's be realistic," she said. "Although it's very likely, we still don't have any solid proof that Cooper didn't kill himself. And it won't be hard to find a lot of people who had a good reason to want that man dead. I'm sure even you two are pleased that he's gone."

"You're right, ma'am," said Inspector Evans. "And although we've collected some statements from the people nearest to him today, it will take a few days to compare what they've said against whatever evidence there is."

↯ Let's call it a day.	Machen wir Feierabend.

"Right," she said. "So **let's call it a day** and enjoy what's left of the weekend."

Inspector Checchino remained quiet and followed Inspector Evans out of the superintendent's office.

Übung 8: Pronouns. Ersetzen Sie die markierten Wörter durch die entsprechenden Pronomen!

1. **Bruno Tartufo** is even shorter than **Inspector Checchino.**

   ____

2. Kim Watt was nervous when she was talking to **the police.**

   ____

3. **Inspector Checchino** gave **Inspector Evans** a big smile.

   ____

4. Fisher was going to watch **the game** with **her friends.**

   ____

On Monday morning, Inspector Checchino arrived at work a good hour before Inspector Evans. She had not been able to sleep well, and she wanted to see what developments had taken place over the weekend. An **incident room** had been set up at the station to collect all the information related to Stanley Cooper's death. The inspector was in there reading through the reports when her colleague finally turned up.

"So, have you heard?" she asked her colleague, her face red with anger.

"Good morning, Sandra! Nice to see you, too," he said ironically. "It's not like you to be here before me on a Monday."

incident room	Einsatzzentrale
arson attack	Brandanschlag
to go up like a match	brennen wie Zunder

"Sorry. Good morning, Gary," she smiled. "Well, have you?"

"Obviously not," he said. "What have you got for me?"

"To begin with, there was an **arson attack** at Lust late last night. The fire brigade[i] think that someone broke a window and set fire to a can of petrol. You saw all the soft furniture in there: it **went up like a match**. The fire's destroyed everything inside."

> Die meisten englischen Gruppenbezeichnungen können Singular und Plural bilden: **fire brigade(s).** Die Singularform kann aber mit Verben im Plural gebraucht werden, wenn man eher die einzelnen Mitglieder der Gruppe als die Gesamtheit meint: **the fire brigade think ...**

"What?! How did that happen? Didn't we have an officer guarding the club all weekend?"

"Only until the club manager locked up after the forensics team had finished investigating the scene," Inspector Checchino explained. "That was on Saturday evening."

"I see," Inspector Evans said. "And do you have any idea why someone might want to burn down one of Cooper's clubs?"

"Well, it was too late to destroy the evidence. My first thought was that Omar Omari might have had something to do with it, but then I read these."

She passed Inspector Evans a pile of paper.

"Three people in the north of the city have reported the **theft** of their **greyhounds**. Altogether we have six expensive racing dogs to find."

"Why should we care about some kidnapped dogs?" he asked.

Then he remembered.

"I suppose I don't need to ask what connects these animals to Stanley Cooper, should I?"

"Probably not, no," said Inspector Checchino. "The owners race them at Cooper's track in Walthamstow. And, as we learnt on Saturday, Kim Watt is the manager there."

"What do we know about the owners – are they friends?"

"One of them is Kim's brother. The other two were close friends of Cooper's. And when I say 'friends', I mean that both were in his gang."

"Ah. But why would someone **target** the dogs and not the people?" asked the inspector.

theft	Diebstahl
greyhound	Windhund
to target sth.	etw. ins Visier nehmen
prestigious	renommiert
to add insult to injury	eine Sache noch schlimmer machen

"Well, for a start, each greyhound is worth at least £40,000. And all six are meant to be racing at an event tonight, so it will be very bad for business if they aren't there."

"Sorry if I'm being a bit slow," he replied, "but what do these dogs have to do with the fire at Lust? What's the connection?"

Inspector Checchino took the papers back and put them on the desk.

"I think it was a symbolic act," she said. "It's typical for gangs. Just think about it: Lust was Cooper's most **prestigious** nightclub, and it's where all the best DJs went to play. Whoever the killer was, he didn't only want to kill the king, he wanted to destroy his palace, too. Kidnapping the dogs **adds insult to injury** for Cooper's gang. If we find the dogs, we will probably find our killer."

"You may have a good point there, Sandra," he replied. "But I need to wake up properly with a coffee before looking at this more closely. Can I get you one, too?"

Nobody knew exactly how many security cameras there were in the city of London, but there were a lot. There were cameras on every main road and in every underground station; they were also installed on every bus to fight vandalism, terrorism and other crimes.

Übung 9: Vocabulary. Lesen Sie weiter und ergänzen Sie den Text mit den fehlenden Wörtern!

A team of junior officers were watching the camera 1. ______ from all of the night 2. ______ that left Trafalgar Square for Finchley in North London early on Saturday morning. It was a boring job, but it was the only way to find out if Omar Omari was telling the 3. ______ : he had told the police that he could not 4. ______ exactly which bus he had taken, but that he normally got on the 134 or the N13.

Meanwhile, Inspectors Evans and Checchino were **reviewing** the videos from Lust. There was a lot of footage on the **hard disk** from Friday night.
Finally, they saw Bruno Tartufo leave the building just before 5 a.m. The recording was turned off five minutes later.

"I don't believe it!" cried Inspector Evans. "He really did leave the club before Cooper was shot!"
"Hmm...," his colleague said quietly, "but did he return?"
They repeated the last ten minutes of footage in Cooper's office. It was a strange feeling to watch the monitor, Inspector Checchino thought. It was as if one of the dead had come back to life and was walking around the room.
The two detectives watched Cooper point to the door, at which point the short Italian man turned and left the room. Cooper then took out his mobile phone and made a call that lasted only a few seconds. He was smiling. After he put his phone back into his pocket, he **waddled** up to the computer in the corner, looked up at the camera, and the screen went black.
"He turned off the recording himself!" she exclaimed in surprise. "Why would he do that?"

to review	überprüfen
hard disk	Festplatte
to waddle	watscheln
drug trafficker	Drogenhändler
disgusting	ekelhaft, abstoßend

"I'd say it's fairly obvious that he was about to do something he wanted to keep secret," replied Inspector Evans dryly.
"What do you mean?"
"Well, it could have been anything. A secret business deal, a meeting with an important **drug trafficker**... maybe even a meeting with a mystery lady friend?"
Inspector Checchino laughed.
"A mystery woman? Do you really think that someone as unattractive and **disgusting** as Stanley Cooper could manage two women?"
He was about to reply when one of the junior officers shouted across the room: "I've found him!"
She had identified the bus that Omar Omari got onto after work on Saturday morning. The club manager had been correct that it was the 134 to Finchley, but he had got the time wrong. According to the

clock on the screen, it was already 5:30 a.m. when he left Trafalgar Square.
"A whole hour later?" Inspector Checchino thought aloud. "A lot can happen in sixty minutes..."

Übung 10: Idioms. Welche Sätze haben die gleiche Bedeutung? Ordnen Sie zu!

1. ☐ Come off it!	a) We should go home.
2. ☐ Let's call it a day.	b) Don't believe that story!
3. ☐ Don't turn me down.	c) You should accept my offer.
4. ☐ Don't be fooled!	d) Be serious!

4 A Smoking Gun

Inspector Checchino was more patient than Inspector Evans. She told him that it would be a bad idea to rush to visit Omar Omari again. They should wait until there was some solid proof that he had returned to the scene, she said.

"Why do you and Fisher always talk about waiting?" he complained. "We should bring him in for questioning before he disappears!"

In the end, the pair spent most of Monday interviewing the other people who worked at Lust, but it proved to be **pointless**. Everyone had gone home before the manager left, and nobody could remember anything unusual.

pointless	zwecklos
noteworthy	bemerkenswert

Two other officers had spoken with the staff at Cooper's bars and his other clubs. Most of them had very little to say. They all respected their boss a great deal, it seemed – or they were still afraid of him, even though he was dead.

The only **noteworthy** report came from one of the women who worked at the dog track in Walthamstow. When the police asked her about Kim Watt, she said that she had seen her boss smoking outside a bar in Soho at around 3:30 a.m. Kim had forgotten to mention this fact when the inspectors had visited her in Chelsea. According to her own statement, she had stayed at work until shortly after 1 a.m. and then driven back home.

"We should go and speak to her again right away!" Inspector Evans said when he heard the report.

"You wanted to do the same with Omar Omari a few hours ago, Gary," sighed Inspector Checchino. "We can't go around **accusing everyone of** lying to us."

to accuse sb. of sth.	jmd. etw. vorwerfen
skull	Schädel
temple	*hier*: Schläfe
square against	rechtwinkelig zu
trajectory	Flugbahn (eines Geschosses)
trace	Spur
revealing	*hier*: aufschlussreich

"Well, one of them is hiding something," he growled. "At least one of them."

Their conversation was interrupted when the telephone on Inspector Evans' desk rang. It was Vash Singh calling from the forensics department. He said that he had some important news for the investigators.

The two detectives always enjoyed talking to Vash, who could explain things in a lively and interesting way. When they walked into his office this time, Vash was holding a plastic **skull** in one hand and a pencil in the other.

"You should have been an actor," said Inspector Evans. "You'd make a good Hamlet."

"Just take a seat and listen to what I have to tell you," he smiled. "First of all, we can definitely rule out suicide now. Look, the bullet must have gone in at this angle."

He was pointing the pencil at the left **temple**, but it was nowhere near **square against** the skull.

"How can you be sure it was murder?" asked Inspector Checchino. "Stanley Cooper was left-handed, and the revolver in his hand was six inches[i] long. Just look at the **trajectory**."

> Das metrische Maßsystem ist im Englischen nach wie vor nicht in allen Kontexten gebräuchlich. Oft begegnet man deshalb den traditionellen Längenmaßen **inch** (Zoll) und **foot** (Fuß).
> Ein **inch** entspricht dabei 2,54 cm, six inches sind also umgerechnet 15,24 cm.
> Ein **foot** (= 12 inches) entspricht 30,48 cm.

Übung 11: Unscramble the text. Lesen Sie weiter und bringen Sie die folgenden Sätze in die richtige Reihenfolge!

a) He turned to Inspector Checchino, who was staring at the skull.

b) "You're right," he agreed. "I wouldn't try to commit suicide like this. It's too difficult."

c) "I'd either put the gun inside my mouth or hold it here, just above my ear, wouldn't you?"

d) Inspector Evans put his hands in the position that Vash was describing.

1	2	3	4

Inspector Checchino sighed a little.
"I haven't really thought about how I would shoot myself, Gary, but you're both right, yes."
"So," Vash continued, "now you probably think that someone was standing in front of him, and not to his side?"
Inspectors Evans and Checchino both nodded.
"You're wrong!" Vash exclaimed. "Neither Cooper nor the killer were standing up. We found no **traces** of blood near head height in the room, and none on the desk either. But there is something very **revealing** about the few small spots on the back wall of the office."
He showed the inspector a photograph of the bloodstains.
"Take a look. The stains on this picture suggest that Cooper's head was about two feet above the ground when he was shot."

"So he was kneeling?" the inspector asked. "Someone made him **beg** for his life?"
"No, the blood is too low down for that as well," Vash explained. "I think he was lying down, which would also explain the position of the body."
Inspector Evans remembered seeing Cooper's body on the office floor in Lust. It was true that he did not appear to have fallen to the ground: both of his arms were resting on either side of his chest.
"Do you mean the killer was lying on top of him?" he asked.
"That would explain the lipstick on his shirt as well, don't you think?" Vash suggested. "Cherchez la femme!"
The inspectors exchanged looks.

Übung 12: Irregular verbs. Ergänzen Sie die richtige Form des angegebenen Verbs!

1. I tell ____________ her about the news this morning.
2. Before he left, Vash put ____________ the skull on the desk.
3. How much time they spend ____________ on the case so far?
4. She read ____________ the report when he walked into the incident room.

"Did anyone ever find Cooper's mobile phone?" asked Inspector Checchino. "We know that he made a call shortly before he was shot, but we have no idea whose number he dialled. We asked his telephone company and they said that it belongs to a **pay-as-you-go phone** that hasn't been registered."

Vash shook his head.

"We didn't find anything else in the office that could help you," he explained. "Apart from one thing, that is. You haven't asked about the really important **clue** that we're quite excited about."

"What's that?" the two inspectors asked simultaneously.

"Whoever shot Stanley Cooper wanted it to look like a suicide, so they left the gun and the **shell casing** on the scene. Of course there is no licence for the gun, but the bullet was quite rare. The ballistics expert says that fewer than five per cent of revolvers use this type. Interestingly, they're more popular in Eastern Europe. There's a large factory near Warsaw."

"He was killed by a Polish bullet?" asked Inspector Evans, surprised.

to beg	betteln
pay-as-you-go phone	Prepaid-Handy
clue	Hinweis, Spur
shell casing	Patronenhülse
irritated	genervt
stubbornly	stur

"Not necessarily, no. The same bullets are available in Britain as well, but they're not used very much."

"The cleaner is Polish," the inspector continued, ignoring what Vash was saying. "I bet she knows some people in Cooper's gangs, too. I thought it was strange that someone who visits a place like Lust so often knew so little about the people there."

Inspector Checchino smiled at Vash and turned to her colleague with an **irritated** look.

"Will you stop accusing everyone, Gary!" she complained. "First it was Bruno, then Omar, then Kim, and now you want to accuse Helena Kowalska!"

"I want to speak to them all again," he replied **stubbornly**. "We should start with the women. After all, that lipstick on his collar must have come from somewhere."

"But it could have been there for days," Inspector Checchino said. "I don't think Stanley Cooper was the most hygienic man to walk this planet..."

hostess	Gastgeberin
to fail	*hier*: unterlassen
awkward	unangenehm, peinlich
to clear one's throat	sich räuspern

Kim Watt was alone when the detectives arrived at her house early that evening. She opened the door with the same surprised look on her face that they had seen on their previous visit.
"Do you mind if we ask you a few more questions about Friday night, Miss Watt?" asked Inspector Evans.
"Of course not! Please come in," she said.
She led them through the hallway to the large kitchen at the back of the house and offered them a seat at the table.
"Would you like some tea, Officers?" she asked politely.
"Oh, that would be great, thank you!" said Inspector Evans happily.
Inspector Checchino was slightly irritated by the woman trying to be the perfect hostess and kicked her colleague's leg under the table.
"Miss Watt," she began, coming straight to the point, "we have received a report that you were in central London after 3 a.m. on the night that Stanley Cooper was shot. Is there a reason why you failed to tell us this on Saturday?"
Kim put down the kettle and turned to the two inspectors. She was biting her lip nervously and did not say a word.
"I've got nothing to hide," she said after a long pause.
"Please just tell us the truth," said Inspector Evans, who thought that the woman seemed much more natural than she did when they had first met.
"You have to understand that this is something I just couldn't tell you the other day. Not with Bruno right beside me..."

She stopped speaking and took a cigarette out of the box that was lying next to the sink.
"I did go into town after work, it's true. I was going to go to Lust, but Omar told me not to because a lot of the people there know Bruno, and Bruno himself was there all night on Friday. So I went to a salsa bar that I like instead. It's only a few minutes away from Charing Cross, and I waited there until Omar finished work."
"Do you remember what time that was?" asked the inspector.

Übung 13: Translation. Übersetzen Sie die folgenden Sätze ins Englische!

1. Ich habe keine Ahnung, welche Nummer er gewählt hat.

   ____

2. Es gibt eine große Fabrik in der Nähe von Warschau.

   ____

3. Die schlanke Frau errötete, als sie die Nachricht hörte.

   ____

4. Offensichtlich wollte er etwas verbergen.

   ____

"Oh, about 4 a.m.," Kim Watt replied.
There was another **awkward** pause in the conversation. Inspector Evans **cleared his throat**.

"We know that Mr Omari left Trafalgar Square at 5:30 a.m. on the 134 bus to Finchley, Miss Watt," he said. "Can you tell us where you and he were before that time?"
The woman began to **blush**. Her pale cheeks were soon almost as red as her flame-coloured hair.

to blush	rot werden, erröten

"We… we visited a hotel where one of Omar's friends works as a night manager. There are always some empty rooms, and he lets us use one from time to time. It's just a bit of fun!"

5 The Fight for Justice

Superintendent Fisher entered the incident room on Tuesday after she walked past and saw that Inspectors Evans and Checchino were laughing inside.

"What's so funny, you two?" she asked impatiently. "It's been over three days now and you've found more questions than answers!"

The two detectives tried to look serious, but Inspector Evans **burst out laughing** again.

"Sorry ma'am," he said. "It's a private joke."

The superintendent noticed Inspector Checchino lifting her hand from Inspector Evans' shoulder.

"Never mind that," she answered. "You need to **get to the bottom of** this case before these gangs get out of control."

There had been more violence on Monday night. Bruno Tartufo had attacked two of Cooper's henchmen and they were in hospital.

"We're doing our best, ma'am," said Inspector Checchino. "We found out today that both the bar manager and the woman that Cooper was seeing have a solid alibi. They were recorded entering and leaving a hotel."

"Who are your other **suspects**?" asked Superintendent Fisher.

"For a moment we thought the cleaner might have been involved," explained Inspector Evans, smiling slightly. "She has keys to the nightclub, and she's Polish."

to burst out laughing	in Gelächter ausbrechen
to get to the bottom of sth.	etw. auf den Grund gehen
suspect	Verdächtiger

"Polish?"
"Well, like the bullets that Vash told us about," Inspector Evans continued. "But we looked into her background today, and it's true that she and her family have nothing to do with any gangsters as far as we can tell."
Inspector Checchino was trying to give the impression(i) that they had more to work with.
"There's still a big question mark over Bruno Tartufo," she said. "He was the last person on the scene, and nobody can prove his alibi."
"And we are watching him very closely," added Inspector Evans. "He's going to be at Cooper's funeral with the rest of the gang at four o'clock today."

Wendungen mit impression

to give the impression
= den Eindruck vermitteln

to create the impression
= den Eindruck erwecken

to make an impression (on sb.)
= Eindruck machen (auf)

to be under the impression (that) ...
= den Eindruck haben, dass ...

to have/get the impression (that) ...
= den Eindruck haben/ bekommen, dass ...

a lasting impression
= bleibender Eindruck

overall impression
= Gesamteindruck

to do an impression of sb.
= jmd. imitieren

funeral	Beerdigung
search warrant	Durchsuchungsbefehl
permission	Erlaubnis
unmarked car	Zivilfahrzeug der Polizei
crowd	Menschenmenge
mourner	Trauergast
hearse	Leichenwagen

"Fine," the superintendent replied shortly. "Just make sure that nobody sees members of the police attending the funeral of one of London's biggest criminals!"
"Any news about the search warrant, ma'am?" asked Inspector Checchino. "Do we have permission to go to Bruno's house yet?"
"Yes, we should have it ready before the end of the afternoon."
With that, Superintendent Fisher turned around and left the incident room.

Übung 14: Word order. Bringen Sie die Wörter in die richtige Reihenfolge!

1. him accused the she murder of

___

2. does suspect what the like look ?

___

3. afternoon will the she this at 4 p.m. at be funeral

___

___

4. crime bottom you of I the want to get this to

___

___

Inspectors Evans and Checchino drove to the crematorium in an **unmarked car** and waited outside the gates. They arrived half an hour early so that they could watch the crowd.

Some **mourners** were already there; many others soon turned up and formed a long line of black suits and overcoats outside the building.

"I don't like these places at all, Gary," said Inspector Checchino quietly when the **hearse** drove up to the door of the crematorium.

"Nobody likes funerals," he smiled. "But I think we can be pleased that Stanley Cooper has danced his last dance, don't you?"
"I suppose so," she said quietly.
"Come on, Sandra, just think about it. You always said he was a monster. Secretly we both know that he **deserved** whatever happened on Friday night. Remember[i] all those drug-related killings last year? Only someone as **evil** as him could have organized so many **executions**. Omari was right: he had it coming."

Achten Sie auf den Unterschied zwischen **remind** und **remember**!
to remember sth.
= sich erinnern an
to remind sb. of sth.
= jmd. an etw. erinnern

Inspector Checchino was silent and watched six fat men lift the **coffin** onto their shoulders.
"He was behind so many other crimes as well, and we all knew it. How many cases have we worked on over the past few years?"
"…And he always got away," she said, speaking over her colleague.
This conversation was practically a routine, but the tense was now new. Stanley Cooper was history.
"If we're lucky, his gang will be powerless soon," he continued. "I…"
"I feel sick," she said suddenly, interrupting him.
Inspector Evans looked across at her in surprise as she opened the door and stepped out of the vehicle.
"I just need some fresh air," she said, looking back into the car. "The air conditioning in there is making me **nauseous**!"
The inspector watched her walk along the grass with one eye fixed on her long, slim legs. After a moment, he thought he saw two people in the crowd staring at

to deserve	verdienen
evil	böse
execution	Hinrichtung
coffin	Sarg
nauseous	übel

Sandra, too. They looked as if they could have been Bruno Tartufo's brothers.

"I think you've got a couple of **admirers** here," Inspector Evans said when Inspector Checchino finally returned and got into the car.
"What are you talking about?"
"There were two men staring at you, didn't you see?"
"Oh... no, not really. This place is full of criminals today, though, Gary. I'm sure we've met them all before at one time or another."
They sat and waited for the funeral to end. Inspector Evans wanted to see whether any fights would break out between the mourners, or whether any more gangsters would come to cause trouble.
After twenty minutes of near silence, a call came through on the radio. It was a sergeant at the station who had just made an arrest.
"We've caught the person who set fire to Lust, sir!" she said in excitement. "It was Bruno Tartufo's younger brother, Alessio. He says that Cooper's gang has divided into two groups: one led by Bruno and the other by a thug in Walthamstow. This second gang forced him to destroy the club in order to save his family. He's been very helpful so far because he wants us to **protect** him."
"Protect him? What do you mean, we should protect him?"
"From the other gang, sir, but from his brother, too. He says that lately Bruno has been a dangerous man to be around. He's also told us who kidnapped those dogs. **Apparently** Bruno is keeping them in his cellar as some kind of trophy, but he wants to either sell them or shoot them. He sees himself as the next **big cheese**!"
"Let's get going!" said Inspector Checchino. "We should go to Tartufo's house before he gets back from this funeral."

admirer	Bewunderer
arrest	Festnahme, Verhaftung
to protect	(be)schützen
apparently	angeblich, anscheinend
ϟ big cheese	hohes Tier, Boss

Übung 15: Choose the correct alternative. Lesen Sie weiter und unterstreichen Sie die richtige Variante!

Bruno Tartufo owned a large house in Chelsea that was **1.** twice / double as large as Kim Watt's. The two detectives did not yet have the search warrant, but they had a good **2.** reason / ground to believe that a crime was **3.** finding / taking place in the cellar. It **4.** meant / meaned they could go inside.

The old **5.** italian / Italian woman who let them in did not ask many questions. When she said that she did not have a key to the cellar, Inspector Evans kicked **6.** open / up the door without thinking twice.

Immediately six brown dogs ran up the stairs and jumped all over him. One even started to lick his face as if it were a giant ice cream.

During the chaos that followed, Inspector Checchino carefully stepped downstairs into the darkness of the cellar. It was her only chance, and she decided to take it.

She slowly pulled out a small box from her coat pocket and placed it on a table at the far end of the room. It contained around two dozen bullets that she had bought undercover on the black market.

As she turned around to leave the cellar, a hand came out of the shadows and landed on her shoulder.

"Sandra," said a concerned voice, "what the hell are you doing?!"

She looked up at Inspector Evans, who was shaking his head in

disbelief. He had a bad feeling about what she was about to say.
“I was just taking a look at these bullets,” she began.
“Don’t lie to me! I saw you put them there.”
Inspector Checchino paused and looked around the room.
“Gary, we’ve been trying all year to bring Cooper to justice, but he always got away. You know how he **operated**. He always had a **puppet** in place to **take the blame** for what he did. And Bruno is no better – he would kill his own mother.”

concerned	besorgt
to operate	*hier*: vorgehen, arbeiten
puppet	Marionette
to take the blame	den Kopf hinhalten

“I can’t believe this!” he hissed. “That’s not how justice works!”
“Justice? Let me tell you about justice, Gary. I’m sure you don’t remember a young man who committed suicide in Camberwell twelve months ago,” she began.
“No, I can’t say that I do. There are a lot of suicides in London.”
“You’re right, there are. But this wasn’t really a suicide. Everyone just assumed that it was...”
“How can you know that?” he asked. “Who are you talking about?”
“It was a university student,” Inspector Checchino said flatly. “Matthew Puglisi.”

Übung 16: Match-up. Welche der folgenden Satzteile gehören zusammen? Ordnen Sie zu!

1. ☐ You've got him wrapped — a) like Fort Knox.
2. ☐ It's protected — b) any stone unturned.
3. ☐ That just adds — c) around your little finger.
4. ☐ Don't leave — d) insult to injury.

to squeeze	drücken
death threat	Morddrohung
to go a long way	*hier*: eine große Hilfe sein
to let sth. go	*hier*: etw. auf sich beruhen lassen

Inspector Evans looked her in the eye. He moved his hand down from her shoulder to her hand and **squeezed** it.
"He wasn't just a student, was he?" he asked calmly.
"No, Gary," she said and looked down at the floor. "He... he was my nephew. He was killed one year ago on Friday night."
Inspector Checchino looked back up at Inspector Evans with tears in her eyes.
"He was my nephew, and he told me that he was in trouble with some drug dealers at a nightclub in Charing Cross. I think you can guess which one. He'd even received some **death threats**, but he was too afraid to talk to the police – apart from me, that is."
"Are you serious? You were behind the whole thing?"
She thought of the two men at the funeral. They were her cousins, and they had helped to arrange her meeting with Cooper.
"Yes, Gary, just little old me. Cooper let me into the club because he thought he was going to get some information about his enemies... it was easy. A little charm and a little lipstick **go a long way**. And I thought it would be easy to blame Tartufo. You know it would."
"Sandra, you must realize that I can't **let it go**," he said.
"You can do whatever you want," she replied quietly.
She was now the one squeezing his hand.
Inspector Evans took a deep breath and sighed.
Inspector Checchino was his friend, but a murder was a murder.
"We can't all go out there and take an eye for an eye!" he cried. "We have Alessio Tartufo now. He will tell us everything we need so that we can arrest his brother. As for you, what can I say?"
"I'm sure you'll do whatever you think is right, Gary."
He growled and went back upstairs, leaving Inspector Checchino in the dark.

Abschlusstest

Lösungen

Glossar

Verzeichnis der Übungen

Abschlusstest

Übung 1: Plural forms. Bilden Sie die richtigen Pluralformen!

1. Peter watched the **cat** eating **a mouse**.

   ____

2. Stanley Cooper's **henchman** was in hospital.

   ____

3. **He** poured **himself** another whisky.

   ____

4. **Her** lifeless **body** was lying on the cold kitchen floor.

   ____

Übung 2: Opposites. Welche Gegenteile gehören zusammen?

1. ☐ innocent	a) neat
2. ☐ jovially	b) doubtful
3. ☐ convinced	c) shabby
4. ☐ posh	d) guilty
5. ☐ littered	e) matter-of-factly

Übung 3: Vocabulary quiz. Lösen Sie das Kreuzworträtsel!

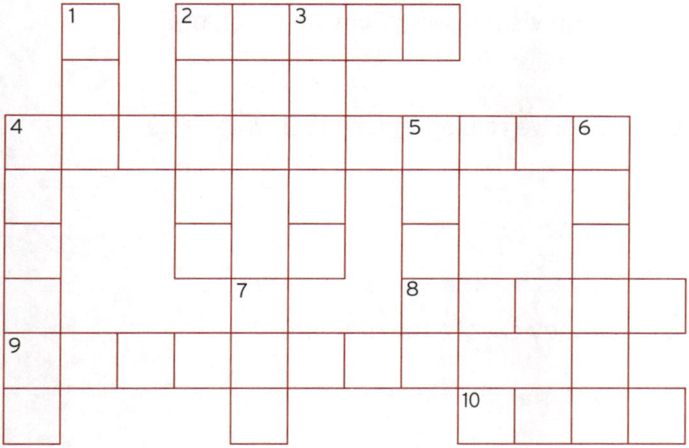

Down

1. Peter is Catherine Wallis' next of ...
2. A group of many people
3. The opposite of "late"
4. Whole
5. An extraordinarily tall person
6. They live in haunted houses
7. Unusual or abnormal

Across

2. A board game played with black and white pieces
4. Motivating
8. A sound or many loud sounds
9. Someone who lives in a certain city or town
10. Very interested in other people's business

Übung 4: Negatives. Verneinen Sie die folgenden Sätze!

1. Why is John visiting Miss Giles this evening?

   ____

2. Peter can drive to Llanprid every day, can't he?

   ____

3. I need some fresh air.

   ____

4. We've already caught the murderer.

   ____

Übung 5: Idioms. Kennen Sie die Bedeutung dieser Redewendungen? Wählen Sie die richtige Antwort!

1. The old lady's face lit up.
   - a) ❒ The old lady's face turned red with anger.
   - b) ❒ The old lady became very cheerful.

2. Long time, no see!
   - a) ❒ We haven't seen each other for a long time!
   - b) ❒ Let's hope we don't see that person again for a long time!

3. The inspector was lost for words.
   - a) ❒ The inspector could not believe what he had heard.
   - b) ❒ The inspector did not want to speak.

4. This adds insult to injury.
   - a) ❒ This helps to lessen the hurt.
   - b) ❒ This makes the situation worse.

Übung 6: Translation quiz. Übersetzen Sie und enträtseln Sie das Lösungswort!

1. Rinder □ _ _ _ _ _
2. Pensionierung _ _ _ _ □ _ _ _ _ _
3. heftiger Streit _ □ _
4. schrecklich _ □ _ _ _
5. leiden _ _ _ _ _ □
6. unerhört □ _ _ _ □ _ _ _ _ _
7. Mädchenname _ _ _ □ _ _   _ _ _ _
8. Strömung □ _ _ _ _ _ _
9. Ufer _ □ _ _
10. Vorwürfe _ _ _ _ □ _ _ _ _ _ _
11. Kleidungsstück _ _ _ _ _ _ □
12. See (schott.) □ _ _ _
13. Vorgehensweise _ _ _ _ □ _ _ _ _

Lösung: □□□□□□□□ □□□□□□

Übung 7: Unscramble. Ordnen Sie die Buchstaben zu einem sinnvollen Wort!

1. ginwadr moro ____________________
2. ayrribl ____________________
3. drumer ____________________
4. idicesu ____________________

Übung 8: True or false? Kreuzen Sie die richtigen Aussagen an!

1. Vash Singh always knew that Cooper was murdered. ❒
2. There was not a lot of blood on the office walls in Lust. ❒
3. The bullets found with the gun are quite common. ❒
4. Catherine Wallis had painted her cottage pink. ❒
5. Cyril Rogers killed Catherine Wallis. ❒
6. Grace Tate had blackmailed her son's wife Joanne. ❒

Übung 9: Translation. Übersetzen Sie folgende Sätze ins Englische!

1. Er will dem Fall auf den Grund gehen.

   ____

2. Es ist mir egal, das hat sie verdient.

   ____

3. Lassen Sie sich nicht täuschen, Frau Inspektorin!

   ____

4. Sein Schnurrbart sieht aus wie eine tote Raupe.

   ____

Lösungen

Death Comes Knocking

Übung 1: **1.** doorbell **2.** surprise **3.** front **4.** neighbours

Übung 2: **1.** Is everything all right? **2.** just in case **3.** a familiar voice **4.** the china plates

Übung 3: **1.** b **2.** b **3.** a **4.** b

Übung 4: arrived (departed), on the side (in the middle), interested (bored), in front of (behind), afterwards (before), shaking his head (nodding)

Übung 5: **1.** Miss Giles called the ambulance.
2. A man dressed in black who is at least six feet tall.
3. Inspector Davies is thinner than Sergeant Jones.
4. Miss Giles read Catherine's tea leaves.

Übung 6: **1.** d **2.** a **3.** b **4.** c

Übung 7: **1.** accidentally **2.** skeleton **3.** unlock **4.** excited

Übung 8: **1.** are searching **2.** works **3.** has/had investigated **4.** have been reading

Übung 9: **1.** nodding **2.** voice **3.** carrying **4.** forensics **5.** neighbour

Übung 10: **1.** pansy **2.** crowd **3.** windowsill **4.** injury **5.** accuse **6.** offend
Lösung: police

Übung 11: **1.** d **2.** b **3.** a **4.** c

Übung 12: **1.** We'll have the letter examined tomorrow.
2. He wanted to keep her company yesterday evening.
3. Shall I put the kettle on now?
4. Unfortunately the old lady has very bad eyesight.

Übung 13: **1.** heavily, heaviness **2.** suspiciously, suspicion **3.** helplessly, helplessness **4.** innocently, innocence

Übung 14: **1.** on **2.** told **3.** could have **4.** had said

Übung 15: **1.** sergeant **2.** her **3.** stairs **4.** time

Übung 16: **1.** What **2.** How **3.** When **4.** How

Crowroad Castle

Übung 1: **1.** window **2.** castle **3.** moment **4.** stepmother **5.** understatement

Übung 2: **1.** b **2.** d **3.** a **4.** c

Übung 3: **1.** dabbed, dabbed **2.** got, got/gotten **3.** went, gone **4.** saw, seen **5.** wore, worn

Übung 4: **1.** c **2.** a **3.** d **4.** b

Übung 5: **1.** everybody **2.** hours **3.** straight **4.** defending

Übung 6:
1. Who / Georgina Tate was closest to the murder victim.
2. Where / They interrogated the Tates in the drawing room.
3. What / The butler was fired.
4. Whose / The butler's handwriting was on the note.

Übung 7: **1.** in **2.** near **3.** at **4.** under

Übung 8: **1.** uneasily **2.** directly **3.** explain to **4.** leapt

Übung 9: **1.** swear **2.** cry **3.** stunned **4.** panicked **5.** exclaim

Übung 10: **1.** awful **2.** innocent **3.** act **4.** along **5.** wellingtons **6.** chase **7.** exactly
Lösung: wealthy

Übung 11: **1.** court **2.** cheap **3.** surprising **4.** aching

Übung 12: **1.** movements **2.** stood up **3.** handshake **4.** habit **5.** sigh

Übung 13: **1.** slowly **2.** sceptically **3.** fast **4.** well

Übung 14: **1.** quarrelling **2.** retreat **3.** suspicious **4.** obvious

Übung 15: **1.** protest **2.** castle **3.** policemen **4.** garment

Übung 16: **1.** Lara agreed with her grandmother. **2.** James thinks his daughter is becoming more and more like her grandmother. **3.** Lara got very angry with her because she told the police that Lara had left the drawing room. **4.** Joanne used to be a high-class call girl.

A Bullet to the Brain

Übung 1: **1.** b **2.** a **3.** a **4.** b

Übung 2: **1.** d **2.** c **3.** a **4.** b

Übung 3: **1.** in **2.** of **3.** from **4.** of **5.** at **6.** off

Übung 4: **1.** rumours **2.** recently **3.** collar **4.** unusual

Übung 5: **1.** Yes, she does. **2.** No, he didn't. **3.** Yes, he was. **4.** No, there isn't.

Übung 6: **1.** access **2.** evidence **3.** guard **4.** stain

Übung 7: **1.** accept **2.** faithful **3.** arrive **4.** bored **5.** smile
Lösung: alibi

Übung 8:
1. He is even shorter than her.
2. Kim Watt was nervous when she was talking to them.
3. She gave him a big smile.
4. Fisher was going to watch it with them.

Übung 9: **1.** footage **2.** buses **3.** truth **4.** remember

Übung 10: **1.** d **2.** a **3.** c **4.** b

Übung 11: **1.** d **2.** b **3.** a **4.** c

Übung 12: **1.** told **2.** had put **3.** have they spent **4.** was reading

Übung 13:
1. I have no idea which number he dialled.
2. There is a large factory near Warsaw.
3. The slim woman blushed when she heard the news.
4. He obviously wanted to hide something.

Übung 14:
1. She accused him of the murder.
2. What does the suspect look like?
3. She will be at the funeral at 4 p.m. this afternoon.
4. I want you to get to the bottom of this crime.

Übung 15: **1.** twice **2.** reason **3.** taking **4.** meant **5.** Italian **6.** open

Übung 16: **1.** c **2.** a **3.** d **4.** b

Abschlusstest

Übung 1: **1.** Peter watched the cats eating mice.
2. Stanley Cooper's henchmen were in hospital.
3. They poured themselves another whisky.
4. Their lifeless bodies were lying on the cold kitchen floor.

Übung 2: **1.** d **2.** e **3.** b **4.** c **5.** a

Übung 3:

	1 K		2 C	H	3 E	S	S				
	I		R		A						
4 E	N	C	O	U	R	A	5 G	I	N	6 G	
N			W		L		I			H	
T			D		Y		A			O	
I				7 O			8 N	O	I	S	E
9 R	E	S	I	D	E	N	T			T	
E				D				10 N	O	S	Y

Übung 4: **1.** Why isn't John visiting Miss Giles this evening?
2. Peter can't drive to Llanprid every day, can he?
3. I don't need any fresh air.
4. We haven't caught the murderer yet.

Übung 5: **1.** b **2.** a **3.** a **4.** b

Übung 6: **1.** cattle **2.** retirement **3.** row **4.** awful **5.** suffer **6.** outrageous **7.** maiden name **8.** current **9.** bank **10.** accusations **11.** garment **12.** loch **13.** procedure
Lösung: Crowroad Castle

Übung 7: **1.** drawing room **2.** library **3.** murder **4.** suicide

Übung 8: **1.** falsch (At first Vash thinks it could be suicide.) **2.** richtig **3.** falsch (The bullets are very rare.) **4.** richtig **5.** falsch (John Bidderscum killed her.) **6.** richtig

Übung 9: **1.** He wants to get to the bottom of the case.
2. I don't care, she had it coming.
3. Don't be fooled, Inspector!
4. His moustache looks like a dead caterpillar.

Glossar

ϟ = umgangssprachlich

access	Zugang
accidentally	versehentlich, unbeabsichtigt
to accompany	begleiten
accusation	Anschuldigung
to accuse sb. of sth.	jmd. etw. vorwerfen
to ache	schmerzen
achievements	Leistungen
to add insult to injury	eine Sache noch schlimmer machen
admirer	Bewunderer
aerial	Antenne
agitatedly	aufgeregt, aufgewühlt
to annoy sb.	jmd. ärgern, nerven
apparently	anscheinend, angeblich
to approach	sich nähern
arson attack	Brandanschlag
as far as I'm concerned	was mich betrifft
awfully	furchtbar
awkward	unangenehm, peinlich
bad luck	Pech
bank	*hier*: Ufer

ϟ battle-axe	Dragoner, (alter) Drachen
to be lost for words	sprachlos sein
to be off	*hier*: weggehen
to bear (bore, borne) sth.	*hier*: etw. ertragen
to beg	betteln
ϟ big cheese	hohes Tier, Boss
bin	Mülleimer
ϟ bitch	Schlampe
to blackmail sb.	jmd. erpressen
to blame sb.	jmd. beschuldigen
to blame sb. for sth.	*hier*: jmd. etw. verübeln
blazing row	furchtbarer Streit
to blink	blinzeln
blow	Schlag
blurred	*hier*: beschlagen
to blush	rot werden, erröten
bolt of lightning	Blitz
to bother sb.	*hier*: jmd. beschäftigen
to bring to justice	zur Rechenschaft ziehen
to burst into	hineinstürzen
to burst out laughing	in Gelächter ausbrechen
cane	Spazierstock
cardigan	Strickjacke
case file	Fallakte
ϟ to catch sb.'s eye	jmd. auffallen
caterpillar	Raupe
cattle	Rinder, Vieh
to change hands	den Besitzer wechseln
chess	Schach
chest	Brust

china	Porzellan
to clear one's throat	sich räuspern
cloakroom	Garderobe
close-knit community	enge Gemeinschaft
clue	Hinweis, Spur
cobweb	Spinnennetz
coffin	Sarg
collar	Halsband; Kragen
⚡ Come off it!	Ach was! / Red doch keinen Unsinn!
to commit a crime	ein Verbrechen begehen
to compete	wetteifern
concerned	besorgt
to conclude	*hier*: schlussfolgern
conspiratorially	verschwörerisch
convenient	günstig, passend
convinced	überzeugt
coroner	Gerichtsmediziner(in)
council house	Sozialwohnung
to crackle	knacken, knistern
crime lord	Verbrecherkönig
crime scene	Tatort
current	Strömung
to curse	fluchen
to dab	abtupfen
to dart	huschen
deaf	taub
death threat	Morddrohung
the deceased	der/die Verstorbene
deck	*hier*: Kartenspiel

to deserve	verdienen
desperation	Verzweiflung
despicable bunch	abscheulicher Haufen
to die of natural causes	eines natürlichen Todes sterben
ϟ to disappear into thin air	sich in Luft auflösen
disapproving	missbilligend
disgusting	ekelhaft, abstoßend
to distract	ablenken
divorce	Scheidung
to divorce	sich scheiden lassen
dog track	Hunderennbahn
Don't be fooled.	Lass dich nicht täuschen.
Don't leave any stone unturned.	Lasst nichts unversucht!
doubt	Zweifel
to down sth. in one	etw. auf ex trinken
to downgrade	herabstufen, degradieren
drawing room	Salon, Wohnzimmer
dread	Grauen
dreadful	schrecklich
to drown sb.	jmd. ertränken
drug trafficker	Drogenhändler
early retirement	Frührente
economically	wirtschaftlich, sparsam
elaborate	kunstvoll
to emphasize	betonen, deutlich machen
to encourage	ermutigen
encouragingly	ermutigend
entire	ganz, gesamt

evidence	Beweis(e)
to exaggerate	übertreiben
exaggerated	übertrieben
to exclaim	ausrufen
executor	Testamentsvollstrecker, Nachlassverwalter
to express	ausdrücken
expressionless(ly)	ausdruckslos
to fail	*hier*: unterlassen
faithful	treu
family feud	Familienfehde
family liaison officer	Opferschutzbeamter
fashionable	in Mode, modisch
fibre	Faser
firm	fest
ϟ fishy	verdächtig
to fit sth.	etw. einbauen
to flash	funkeln, blitzen
flashing	blinkend, aufleuchtend
flatly	ausdruckslos
to flick through	durchblättern
to flinch	zusammenzucken
to float	treiben, schwimmen
ϟ folks	Leute
forced entry	gewaltsames Eindringen
forensics	Spurensicherung
frail	gebrechlich
to freeze (froze, frozen)	*hier*: erstarren
to frown	die Stirn runzeln
ϟ fruity	verrückt, flott

funeral	Beerdigung
furious	sehr wütend
to gain	gewinnen (an), profitieren
garment	Kleidungsstück
to gasp	keuchen, nach Luft schnappen
to get hold of sb.	jmd. erreichen
to get to the bottom of sth.	etw. auf den Grund gehen
to give out	*hier*: von sich geben
to give way	nachgeben, einknicken
to glower	finster blicken
to go a long way	*hier*: eine große Hilfe sein
ϟ good-for-nothing	Nichtsnutz
to gossip	tratschen
to go up like a match	brennen wie Zunder
to grab	packen, greifen
grand	erhaben
gravel drive	Kiesauffahrt
greyhound	Windhund
the Grim Reaper	der Sensenmann
to groan	stöhnen
to growl	brummen
to grumble	murren, brummen
guilty	schuldig
gulp	(großer) Schluck
hanging basket	Blumenampel
hard disk	Festplatte
haunted castle	Spukschloss
to have a row	heftig streiten, Krach haben
to head for	*hier*: zusteuern auf

hearse	Leichenwagen
heart failure	Herzversagen
hedge	Hecke
He had that coming.	Das hat er verdient.
henchman, -men *pl*	Scherge, Handlanger
to hiss	zischen, fauchen
to hobble	hinken
hood	Kapuze
horrible sight	schrecklicher Anblick
hostess	Gastgeberin
How dare you!	Wie können Sie es wagen!
impression	Eindruck
impressive	beeindruckend
in an uproar	in Aufruhr
in charge of	zuständig für
incident	Vorfall, Ereignis
incident room	Einsatzzentrale
in court	vor Gericht
injury	Verletzung
to insist	beharren, bestehen auf
insult	Beleidigung
to intend	beabsichtigen
intercom	Gegensprechanlage
to interrogate	befragen, verhören
to intimidate	einschüchtern
in vain	vergeblich
investigation	Ermittlung, Untersuchung
investigator	Ermittler(in)
irritated	genervt

ϟ jolly good	prima, hervorragend
jovially	fröhlich, herzlich
judging by ...	nach ... zu urteilen
ϟ to jump out of one's skin	erschreckt hochfahren
to keep in touch	in Verbindung bleiben
Keep me posted!	Halte mich auf dem Laufenden!
to knit	stricken
ϟ lad	Bursche, Junge
landing stage	Bootssteg
late	*hier*: (kürzlich) verstorben
laundry basket	Wäschekorb
to leap (leapt, leapt)	springen
ϟ Let's call it a day.	Machen wir Feierabend.
to let sth. go	*hier*: etw. auf sich beruhen lassen
to light (lit, lit) up	*hier*: aufleuchten, strahlen
like Fort Knox	wie eine Festung
lined with	gesäumt von
littered with	übersät mit
loch	See (Schottland)
loft	Dachboden
ϟ Long time, no see!	Lange nicht gesehen!
maiden name	Mädchenname
to make the most of sth.	das Beste machen aus
marble	Marmor
matter-of-factly	nüchtern, sachlich
to mock	spotten
mortuary	Leichenhalle
mourner	Trauergast

moustache	Schnurrbart
muddy puddle	Schlammpfütze
to mutter	murmeln, nuscheln
napkin	Stoffserviette
nauseous	übel
neatly	ordentlich, sauber
neatly stored	sauber aufgeräumt
newly-wed	frisch verheiratet
next of kin	nächste(r) Angehörige(r)
niece	Nichte
nosy	neugierig
noteworthy	bemerkenswert
notorious	berüchtigt
to nudge	anstubsen
oak	Eiche
to object	einwenden
to observe	beobachten
to offend sb.	jmd. beleidigen
ominously	unheilvoll
only child	Einzelkind
to operate	*hier*: vorgehen, arbeiten
operator	Telefonist(in)
to outdo (-did, -done) sb.	jmd. übertreffen
outrageous	unerhört
to overhear (-heard, -heard)	zufällig mithören
pacemaker	Herzschrittmacher
pansy	Stiefmütterchen
to pant	keuchen
paramedic	Rettungssanitäter(in)
passer-by	Passant(in)

pay-as-you-go phone	Prepaid-Handy
peculiar	seltsam
permission	Erlaubnis
pigsty	Schweinestall
plump	pummelig
pointless	zwecklos
pointy	spitz
to poke	stechen
posh	vornehm, schick
to pour sb. sth.	jmd. etw. einschenken
prejudiced	voreingenommen
prestigious	renommiert
to pretend	so tun, als ob; vorgeben
procedure	Vorgehensweise
to protect	(be)schützen
to prove	beweisen
puppet	Marionette
purpose in life	Lebensziel
to put the final touches to sth.	etw. den letzten Schliff geben
to put the kettle on	Wasser aufsetzen
to put up with sth.	etw. tolerieren
quarrelling	Streiten
to radio	(an)funken
to read sb.'s mind	jds. Gedanken lesen
to read sb.'s palm	jmd. aus der Hand lesen
reassuringly	beruhigend
recording	Aufnahme
to recreate	nachbilden
redhead	Rothaarige(r)

reluctantly	widerwillig, widerstrebend
residents	Einwohner
to retreat	sich zurückziehen
revealing	*hier*: aufschlussreich
to review	überprüfen
rightfully	rechtmäßig
to rip sth. off	etw. ab-, wegreißen
rockery	Steingarten
to rule out	ausschließen
to rummage around	herumwühlen
rumour	Gerücht
run-down	heruntergekommen
to run sb. over	jmd. überfahren
ruthless	umbarmherzig
sample	Probe, Muster
screeching brakes	quietschende Bremsen
↯ to screw up one's nose	die Nase rümpfen
scythe	Sense
search warrant	Durchsuchungsbefehl
security camera footage	Aufnahmen der Überwachungskameras
seductive	verführerisch
sensible	vernünftig
to settle differences	Differenzen beilegen
severed	abgetrennt
shabby	schäbig
shade	*hier*: Farbton, Schattierung
shaky	zittrig
shape	Gestalt, Form
sheepishly	einfältig

shell casing	Patronenhülse
to shrug	die Achseln zucken
to shuffle	schlurfen
to sigh	seufzen
sip	Schlückchen
skull	Schädel
to slam	zuschlagen
slave	Sklave/Sklavin
to slip	*hier*: entgleiten, nachlassen
ϟ slut	Schlampe
smart	*hier*: schick
smooth	glatt
to snap	*hier*: blaffen
to sniff at sth.	an etw. riechen
to snigger	(hämisch) kichern
ϟ to snuff it	draufgehen, abkratzen
to sob	schluchzen
solemn(ly)	düster, ernst
solid proof	eindeutige Beweise
to sort out	*hier*: in Ordnung bringen
spark	Funke
ϟ spinster	unverheiratete Frau, alte Jungfer
to spit (spat, spat)	*hier*: fauchen
square against	rechtwinkelig zu
to squeeze	drücken
stain	Fleck
to stammer	stammeln, stottern
to startle sb.	jmd. erschrecken
to state	feststellen

steady	*hier*: ruhig
sternly	streng
sticky	klebrig
stiff	steif
to stroke	streichen über, streicheln
stubbornly	stur
substantial	bedeutend, stichhaltig
to suffer	leiden
suicide	Selbstmord
suit of armour	Ritterrüstung
superior	Vorgesetzte(r)
to suppose	annehmen, vermuten
suspect	Verdächtige(r)
suspicious	verdächtig
to swallow	schlucken
to swap	tauschen
to sway	sich wiegen, schwanken
sweat	Schweiß
swiftly	rasch, schnell
ϟ swine	Schweinehund
sympathy	Mitgefühl
ϟ take sb. in	jmd. festnehmen
to take the blame	den Kopf hinhalten
to target sth.	etw. ins Visier nehmen
ϟ tart	*hier*: Nutte, Schlampe
tart(ly)	bissig, mit scharfer Zunge
temple	*hier*: Schläfe
terrified	entsetzt
theft	Diebstahl
to think straight	klar denken

threat	Drohung, Bedrohung
thug	Schläger(typ)
to tire of doing sth.	müde werden, etw. zu tun
tool	Werkzeug
trace	Spur
tracksuit trousers	Trainingshose
trainers	*hier*: Turnschuhe
trajectory	Flugbahn (eines Geschosses)
trembling	zitternd
to turn sb. down	jmd. einen Korb geben
to turn sth. down	etw. ablehnen
two-way mirror	Einwegspiegel
uneasy	unangenehm, ungut
unmarked car	Zivilfahrzeug (der Polizei)
unmistakable, -ably	unverwechselbar
unshaven	unrasiert
to upset (upset, upset) sth.	etw. umkippen, umwerfen
valuable	wertvoll
vest (GB)	Unterhemd
violence	Gewalt
to waddle	watscheln
to wade	waten
waste of time	Zeitverschwendung
weeds *pl*	Unkraut
wellingtons	Gummistiefel
wickedly	boshaft
will	Testament
windowsill	Fensterbank
to wipe	abwischen
witch	Hexe

to witness	miterleben, Zeuge sein von
to wonder	sich fragen
word had spread	es hatte sich herumgesprochen
to wrap around	wickeln um
wrinkly	runzlig
You can say that again!	Das kannst du laut sagen!

Verzeichnis der Übungen

Death Comes Knocking

The Secret of Crowroad Castle

	Schwerpunkt	Übung	Seite
1	Wortschatz	Fill in the blanks	47
2	Wortschatz	Opposites	50
3	Grammatik	Verb forms	51
4	Wortschatz	Synonyms	54
5	Wortschatz	Choose the correct word	57
6	Textverständnis	Questions to the text	60
7	Wortschatz	Prepositions	63
8	Wortschatz	Synonyms	65
9	Wortschatz	Emphasis	67
10	Wortschatz	Translation quiz	68
11	Wortschatz	Odd one out	71
12	Wortschatz	Translation	73
13	Grammatik	Adverbs	75
14	Wortschatz	Translation	77
15	Wortschatz	Unscramble	80
16	Textverständnis	Questions to the text	83

A Bullet to the Brain

1	Grammatik	Multiple choice	88
2	Wortschatz	Synonyms	91
3	Grammatik	Prepositions	93
4	Wortschatz	Unscramble	95
5	Textverständnis	Short answers	99
6	Wortschatz	Odd one out	101
7	Wortschatz	Opposites quiz	104
8	Grammatik	Pronouns	105
9	Wortschatz	Fill in the blanks	108
10	Wortschatz	Idioms	110
11	Textverständnis	Unscramble the text	113
12	Grammatik	Irregular verbs	114
13	Wortschatz	Translation	117
14	Grammatik	Word order	121
15	Wortschatz	Choose the correct alternative	124
16	Wortschatz	Match up the phrases	125

Compact Lernkrimis auch in Spanisch, Französisch, Italienisch und Deutsch erhältlich.

Compact Lernkrimi Classic

A1

A2

B1

Das Rätsel der Mumie
ISBN 978-3-8174-7304-5

Die Jagd nach dem Vampir
ISBN 978-3-8174-7305-2

Game Over in Soho
ISBN 978-3-8174-7878-1

Im Schatten des Towers
ISBN 978-3-8174-7687-9

Schüsse im Nebel
ISBN 978-3-8174-7763-0

Toxic Testament
ISBN 978-3-8174-7879-8

American English

Tod im Grand Canyon
ISBN 978-3-8174-7572-8

Sammelband 3 in 1 (B1/B2)

Inspector Hudson ermittelt
ISBN 978-3-8174-7625-1

London Crime Time
ISBN 978-3-8174-7787-6

B2

Das geheimnisvolle Gemälde
ISBN 978-3-8174-7306-9

Die Spur des Höllenhundes
ISBN 978-3-8174-7307-6

Diebstahl im Morgengrauen
ISBN 978-3-8174-7638-1

Lady Mayfairs Rache
ISBN 978-3-8174-7815-6

Business English

Das letzte Roulette
ISBN 978-3-8174-7609-1

Der 25-Millionen-Dollar-Coup
ISBN 978-3-8174-7659-6

Schmierige Geschäfte
ISBN 978-3-8174-7658-9

Teuflische Intrigen
ISBN 978-3-8174-7608-4

American English

Das Skyline-Syndikat
ISBN 978-3-8174-7573-5

C1 / C2

Compact Lernkrimi Kurzkrimis	Compact Lernkrimi Mystery	Compact Lernkrimi Thriller	
			A1
Blood and Breakfast ISBN 978-3-8174-7760-9 **Endstation Waterloo Bridge** ISBN 978-3-8174-7733-3 **Es war Mord, my Lord** ISBN 978-3-8174-7734-0 **Mord at Teatime** ISBN 978-3-8174-7839-2			A2
Death Comes Knocking ISBN 978-3-8174-7945-0	**Der rote Nebel** ISBN 978-3-8174-7574-2	**Ein fast perfekter Coup** ISBN 978-3-8174-7568-1 **Komplott unter Palmen** ISBN 978-3-8174-7571-1	B1
	Der Seelenjäger ISBN 978-3-8174-7581-0	**Die genetische Falle** ISBN 978-3-8174-7569-8 **Schatten der Vergangenheit** ISBN 978-3-8174-7570-4	B2
			C1 / C2

Compact Lernkrimi History

Compact Lernkrimi Hörbuch

	Compact Lernkrimi History	Compact Lernkrimi Hörbuch
A1		
A2		
B1	**Der Rächer von Canterbury** ISBN 978-3-8174-7662-6 **Tod eines Dandys** ISBN 978-3-8174-7660-2	**Das Mädchen von King's Cross** ISBN 978-3-8174-7673-2 **Der Themse-Mörder** ISBN 978-3-8174-7674-9
B2	**Der unheimliche Ritter** ISBN 978-3-8174-7661-9 **Die Rache des Lords** ISBN 978-3-8174-7663-3	**Blutige Erbschaft** ISBN 978-3-8174-7676-3 **Die Intrigantin** ISBN 978-3-8174-7675-6 **Business English** **Mord im Office** ISBN 978-3-8174-7747-0
C1 / C2		

Compact Lernkrimi
Audio-Learning

Compact Lernkrimi
Sprachkurs

	Englisch für Anfänger (A1/A2) ISBN 978-3-8174-7784-5	**A1**
Verschollen im Dartmoor ISBN 978-3-8174-7796-8		**A2**
Totenstille im Hyde Park ISBN 978-3-8174-7797-5		**B1**
		B2
		C1 / C2